MILITARY HISTORY FROM PRIMARY SOURCES

INTO BATTLE WITH NAPOLEON 1812

THE JOURNAL OF JAKOB WALTER,
A NAPOLEONIC FOOT SOLDIER 1806-1812

Edited and annotated by Bob Carruthers

Pen & Sword
MILITARY

This edition published in 2013 by
Pen & Sword Military
An imprint of
Pen & Sword Books Ltd
47 Church Street
Barnsley
South Yorkshire
S70 2AS

First published in Great Britain in 2011 in digital format by
Coda Books Ltd.

ISBN 978 1 78159 145 1

Originally published as 'A German Conscript with Napoleon'
Jakob Walter's recollections of the campaigns of 1806-1807, 1809, and 1812-1813
Edited and translated by Otto Springer. Published by the University of Kansas, 1938

A CIP catalogue record for this book is
available from the British Library

Printed and bound by
CPI Group (UK) Ltd, Croydon, CR0 4YY

Pen & Sword Books Ltd incorporates the Imprints of Pen & Sword Aviation, Pen & Sword Family
History, Pen & Sword Maritime, Pen & Sword Military, Pen & Sword Discovery, Pen & Sword
Politics, Pen & Sword Atlas, Pen & Sword Archaeology, Wharncliffe Local History, Wharncliffe
True Crime, Wharncliffe Transport, Pen & Sword Select, Pen & Sword Military Classics, Leo
Cooper, The Praetorian Press, Claymore Press, Remember When, Seaforth Publishing and Frontline
Publishing

For a complete list of Pen & Sword titles please contact
PEN & SWORD BOOKS LIMITED
47 Church Street, Barnsley, South Yorkshire, S70 2AS, England
E-mail: enquiries@pen-and-sword.co.uk
Website: www.pen-and-sword.co.uk

CONTENTS

Prince Eugene under fire by the Moskva river. Evening, September 5th 1812

INTRODUCTION

When we think of the campaigns of Napoleon we naturally tend to consider the army from the point of view of the Frenchmen serving under the eagles. In reality Napoleon's armies were far from homogenous and as the spirit of revolution, combined with a wave of conquests, engulfed Europe a large number of foreign volunteers and conscripts from the German principalities found themselves either by accident or design under the command of one of history's most famous generals. Also in the ranks were Poles, Italians, Bavarians, Wurtembergers, Hessians and representatives from a host of other long vanished kingdoms and principalities which are now united in present day Germany, the Czech Republic and Poland

One of these men was a Westphalian youth called Jakob Walter. Walter was a stonemason by trade and at the age of eighteen had the misfortune to be called to the colours in 1806 and witnessed the Emperor's campaigns of 1806-1807, during which the German forces fought against Prussia. In 1809 Napoleon turned against Austria and in 1812 he turned his gaze towards Russia. Having survived the first two campaigns relatively unscathed, Walter then embarked as a member of the Grand Armée on the invasion of Russia and was witness to the terrible events of the 1812 campaign which very nearly killed him. Walter's Journal is written in very simple terms and in a plain matter of fact style. Through him we begin to gain an understanding of the lot of the Napoleonic foot soldier and above all what it really meant to "march with the Emperor". Walter chronicles for us the thousand of miles which he and others like him tramped around Europe. It is truly astonishing to consider the long marches which he endured in Prussia, Poland and, of course, Russia. However, it was the Russian campaign of 1812 which inevitably left the greatest mark on Walter and this titanic event has also left an enduring influence on the pages of military history.

PORTRAIT OF NAPOLÉON IN IMPERIAL COSTUME 1805
Sketch by Jacques-Louis David (1748–1825)

I have chosen to illustrate this volume with many of the watercolours produced by Albrecht Adam, another German who served in the ranks of Napoleon's armies, who witnessed many of the same scenes as Jakob Walter. Together the text and illustrations provide a powerful primary insight in to the events of 1812 as witnessed by the men who were there.

This translation of Walter's diaries first appeared in 1938. It was originally edited and translated by Otto Springer and was initially published, out of chronological sequence, under the title '" German Conscript with Napoleon – Jakob Walter's Recollections of the Campaigns of 1806-1807, 1809, and 1812-1813."

Thank you for buying this book I hope it brings you as much pleasure as it did for me when I first discovered this unprepossing recollection twenty-five years ago.

Bob Carruthers 2011.

CHAPTER I

In the year 1806, I was drafted with many of my comrades into military service in the conscription at that time and was assigned to the regiment of Romig, which afterward was given the name of Franquemont and of Number 4 and which was in the Ludwigsburg garrison. In the fall I traveled with the regiment to Prussia in the campaign which Emperor Napoleon with the princes, then his allies, was conducting at that time against Prussia. In the fall we marched through Ellwangen, Nuremberg, Ansbach,

Bayreuth, Plauen, Dresden in Saxony, then through Bunzlau into Grossglogau in Silesia, where we remained in garrison for about three weeks.

During a period from the month of January to the month of. March, I had to go with half of the regiment to accompany several convoys of captured Prussians from Glogau back through Crossen, Frankfort-on-the-Oder, and Dresden, where we were relieved. We were given good quarters everywhere, which kept me always healthy and cheerful in spite of the continuous marching. Furthermore, I was only nineteen years old, a fact which caused me frequently to participate in thoughtless and dangerous enterprises. During our return to Glogau the convoy, together with a Bavarian corps, was surrounded by Prussians in Bunzlau. We then closed all the gates and caught the spies.

In this city it happened in my quarter that a comrade wanted to force the landlord to sing. However, he refused to do so, sitting the whole night on a bench near the stove weeping. Since this man could not sing because of his sorrow, Soldier Hummel wanted to frighten him, took his rifle, cocked the hammer, and shot. The bullet passed by me and another soldier and lodged in the wall. I wanted to mention this in order to show how the soldiers were running wild at that time.

A spy who was a village smith was brought before the guard house. He had letters and orders to tell the Prussians of our strength in man power. He was laid on a bench and whipped by two or three corporals. Two men had to hold his feet and two his head. His leather breeches were stretched out and water poured on them, and then he received about one hundred and fifty blows. At last he could no longer speak, because he was half dead. At every blow the lieutenant said to the smith, "This is a Bavarian thaler; this is a Württemberg thaler," at which the lieutenant was really able to laugh. After this experience the smith was taken to the threshing floor [?] and shot. Blows with clubs also were heaped upon many innocent people in this city.

When the Prussians who were laying siege to the city lost their courage, they withdrew, and we entered Glogau again.

After I had been in Glogau one day, I had to escort with a part of the regiment 19 money wagons to the Grand Army. These money wagons were drawn by four and six horses, and many sank into the mire every day. This march went through Breslau and then across the Polish border to Kalisch, Posen, Gnesen, [Inowr] azlav, and Thorn on the Vistula River, where the convoy was given over. From there we had to return to Gnesen, a sizable city in Poland. There we had a storeroom to guard, watching in a room at a bright fire. In this house there was a Polish soldier's wife who taught me as much Polish as I would need. We suffered from the cold a great deal there during the two weeks of our stay because our feet got no warmth and a severely cold winter prevailed.

Finally, eight men, including myself, were sent into the outlying villages by the Commandant of the city. I received several written orders to requisition food supplies; yet, even though I did not know the roads, I was not furnished with a guide. Since I had to carry out my commission, I went, as did my other comrades, into the Jewish section, where everyone spoke German but few could read or write it and few, as I found out, could read Polish. There I wanted to take the first Jew I came across as a guide, but the first escaped and likewise the others I chased. Finally, I ran after one and chased him into the attic of his house and caught him among many women and children. Here he wanted to defend himself, and I had to use force. I took him, dragged him down the two flights of stairs, and had to hold him by the coat and kick him forward for two hours, threatening him if he should fail to lead me to the right village. Here I had to walk through a lake, and the water went over my knees. I commanded the Jew to lead the way, and he howled so loudly for fear of drowning that I had to laugh and send him back immediately. After crossing, the Jew sat down and shook out his water-filled boots.

After I arrived in the village ahead of me, the nobleman quartered me in the mayor's house; but, when I entered the room through a straw door, I could not stand upright and could not see any people for the smoke. This compelled me to quarter myself at the nobleman's house.

The next day I tried to visit eight villages, but I frequently got to only one or two in a day, for often it was necessary to walk a distance of three or four miles. In one manor I once could get no guide, since everyone ran away and hid from my lone self. A big dog also kept attacking me, and I shot the dog because of my customary youthful impulses. This was another reason why I got no guide. Here I traveled alone, depending upon my own good judgment, to a village in another region and received here, as almost everywhere, unrequested presents which pleased me very much.

Since, as I have said, it required eight days instead of four to visit the villages and since the convoy lying in Gnesen left hurriedly, I and three other men returned too late. The convoy was gone. Having obtained the route of march from Gnesen to the Neisse stronghold in Silesia, we had to march alone a distance of about one hundred hours.

Since we four men thought we were well off, we did not hurry to catch the convoy but contented ourselves with comfortable traveling. We visited the noblemen, who usually had to hitch up their own good horses for us while we threatened that we had to catch the convoy by the next day and that the noblemen could be made responsible if we missed it. However, we usually had to combine force with these methods to get horses.

Once we took four horses from a nobleman, and unfortunately the march led us through a large government city, Posen. Here the servant said

MARSHAL BARCLAY DE TOLLY.
Barclay de Tolly is depicted in the common General uniform.
George Dawe 1771-1829

something we could not understand to a few burghers, but we were not stopped. We wanted to drink some brandy in the last suburb, and we halted. At once the nobleman came up on a white horse, being a Polish general stationed there in garrison. Our position did not seem to be the best, and we had to discuss what was to be done. Quickly our sickest-looking comrade had to lie on the ground and continually moan and lament. The general greeted us by threatening to write to our headquarters in Silesia about such use of his horses. That might have happened if the sick man had not aroused some serious doubt on the part of the general. To defend ourselves further, we said we had just as much right to complain to our regiment that His Excellency the general had hindered our progress and had caused the death of a sick man. At these words a wagon with two horses was brought there at once, and we were able to travel away laughing with our healthy "sick man."

After Posen we came into a little Polish town called Fraustadt, which was a garrison town. I have to mention this town because of its windmills, which numbered 99.

From Fraustadt we came after several marches to Glogau on Easter Eve and were quartered with a Jew. Since we were acquainted in this city, we wanted to give this Jew something to remember us by. The meals were usually attended by violence on account of stinginess and uncleanliness; and, since clean chinaware was always set up for the Jews, we took over all that chinaware and ate with it, causing such an uproar in the house that a crowd of people gathered in front of the house to listen. Our defense was that we just had not thought of making anything unkosher that had been intended not to be for us, and so the Jews could not set forth any complaint.

From Glogau we traveled with some of the Black Riflemen toward the stronghold of Schweidnitz. We had not obtained a wagon out of Glogau, which seemed to us a great hardship. It was Easter Day, March 29, and we looked for horses in every stable in a village called Hochkirch, but found none, which failure made it necessary for us to look even in the parsonage.

When we searched the buildings and found nothing but an old woman there, we wanted to look into the church where the service was in progress, and we found the church full of people. Meanwhile there stood in the court a beautiful carriage hitched with two horses; so we untied the horses and rode away without a servant. Since we had to hurry to escape the church folk, I had to drive and ran into a tree stump so that the carriage and all of us lay there in the mud. Here we set out again and traveled until we were a half mile from Schweidnitz. In that place there was a tavern in the forest; and, after we had sold the carriage and horses cheaply to the innkeeper, we continued our march.

When we came to the fortress of Neisse, we had to go on with our regiment and with the Seckendorff Regiment through Breslau, across Poland through the city of Kalisch, then Posen, Gnesen, [Inowr]azlav, and Thorn on the Vistula River.

From there we went through Prussian Pomerania toward the fortress of Colberg on the Baltic Sea. One mile from this stronghold is a town called Belgard, and there was a castle there which had belonged to our King Frederick while he had encamped in this town as general of the cavalry.

On this journey from Thorn to Colberg I saw a lake which lay in a forest by a monastery. In this lake were multitudes of frogs which were of a very beautiful bright blue color, and no soldier would quit until he had caught one of these beautiful frogs. Beyond this region we came to a little town in which the largest part of the inhabitants were Jews. The same day we had had to walk several miles through swamps and snow water up to our knees; and, when quarters were taken there for the evening, I and four other men came into a Jew's house. The room was full of straw and goats.

PRINCE EUGENE, STEPSON OF NAPOLEON, AND COMMANDER OF THE "ARMY OF ITALY," NAPOLEON'S IV CORPS.

In the Russia Campaign Eugene commanded the IV Corps in the Battles of Borodino and Maloyaroslavets. During the retreat from Moscow, Eugene took command of the remnants of the French forces and led them back to Germany in 1813 after Napoleon and Murat had left the main body.

Since neither fire nor wood was to be had, we went into the next house to lodge, looked for the Jew, and took 'him into custody; for only by applying such stern treatment could we induce the wife to bring us food on her husband's account.

While we were besieging the fortress of Colberg, we were assigned a camp in a swampy place. Since wood and even straw were rarely to be had, the barracks were built from earth and sod, and ditches were dug around them.

As some sickness was arising because of the continual fog, I also became sick and had to go to the hospital in the fortress of Stettin, which is also a fortress on the sea. When I arrived with several from the regiment, we were placed three stories high under the roof in the hospital. Here twelve to fifteen of the men about me died every day, which made me sick at my stomach and would have caused my death in the end if I and four comrades had not reported ourselves as being well even on the second day and escaped. This hospital and three others, according to rumor, had six thousand sick people; and that was the reason also why everyone with an appetite had to suffer great hunger, which was one of the things that moved me to leave. The third day we five men were allowed to go, and we traveled without delay to our regiment.

In this fortress of Stettin the Würzburg soldiers were stationed and were all dressed in uniforms of white and red, that is, like Austrian soldiers. This stronghold had a position which could be besieged only by land from the side facing Berlin. Here the Oder River flows into the Baltic Sea. This, together with the swamps, which extend for a mile and through which currents of the Oder flow, surrounds two-thirds of the city. Over the swamp is a paved dike a mile long, reaching to the head of the bridge near a village named Dam. This city is large and beautiful and had especially large merchant ships in the harbor to look at.

When we five men came again without delay to the fortress of Colberg, we had the honor of enduring the siege in good health for another three weeks. Pentecost Night is especially fixed in my memory, since the fortress was stormed then.

When we had to leave camp after midnight, all the regiments marched

MARSHAL MACDONALD.
Serving throughout the French Revolutionary and Napoleonic Wars, he led major formations in the 1809 campaign against Austria, in Spain (1810–1811), Russia (1812), Germany (1813), and in France (1814).

forward through the swamp; and finally, when light firing began upon the outposts, we were commanded to attack by wading through the rampart ditches with fascines, to tread these in, and to scramble up the outworks by chopping and shove ling. When I stood in the ditch, each first soldier had to pull up the next one with his rifle. The ramparts were of sand, and everyone frequently fell back again because of the attack of the enemy, or just because of the sliding sand; yet in that place the huge cannonballs flew by above us [?], thundering so violently that we would have believed the earth would burst to pieces. When everyone was almost on top of the earthwork, the Prussians were slaughtered with great vigor, and the rest took flight into the gate. Then we, too, wanted to gain possession of the gateway in order to enter the city, but at this critical time many of these Prussians were shot along with our men by small and large guns, and the gate was closed.

Since all sorts of shells and rockets broke out of the fortress like a cloudburst, we had to take to flight. Those who meanwhile were scrambling up the outworks had to jump from the fortress into the moat along with their prisoners, and all the rest had to do likewise. During this retreat many fell on bayonets, many drowned, and many of us were also brought into the fortress as prisoners and sent away to Danzig by sea.

When we reached camp, we saw many who had lost their helmet, rifle, saber, knapsack, etc. Because of various falls and pains, many looked for wounds and had none; many, however, did not become aware of the wounds which they had until they reached camp.

In this camp there were Poles, Westphalians, French, and, as mentioned before, only two regiments of us from Württemberg. One morning the Prussians surprised the Polish camp from the sea with their ships, as had happened before on Easter. The cannon fire on the Poles was so heavy that they could not withdraw fast enough. Their cannonballs also traveled

EMPEROR NAPOLEON BONAPARTE, 1812.

Napoleon led the Grande Armée through the Austrian Empire, on to Russia, defeating the Tsar's forces at Maloyaroslavets and Borodino, though ultimately having to retreat from Moscow, due to supply issues. Napoleon's interior lines faltered against the Scorched Earth tactics employed by Russia, preventing French forces to live off the land. This was one of the sources of French effectiveness - there was no need for fixed supply lines, enabling increased rapidity of movement and thus surprise, as best demonstrated in the Ulm Campaign in 1805.

PRINCE EUGÈNE, VICEROY OF ITALY
Andrea Appiani 1754-1817

more than half again as far toward our camp as our balls did across the water, since the surrounding swamps were frozen and the balls could roll along on the ice so fast that one ball often took off the feet and legs of ten or twelve men, frequently both feet of the same man. During this blockade the Prussians frequently made attacks, although every time with great losses.

At the end of over four weeks the command came from General Vandamme, or rather from Prince Jerome, that both regiments from Württemberg should go by forced march to Silesia to the siege of Silberberg.

When we marched away, we had to get additional horses in the little town of Belgard to carry the knapsacks, etc. This brought me to misfortune, since my knapsack, cloak, bayonet, and the money which I had packed in a belt of my cloak, were lost. When I was in my quarters and learned this, I wanted a horse to ride to the other companies in order to look for my lost articles, but I had to make use of a military requisition and look for a horse with my landlord in the forest, since I saw that there was horse manure in the stable. When I had the horse but no saddle or bridle, I made a bridle out of a bit of rope and traveled about three miles in the surrounding villages but found nothing. At best I only got lost and did not know how to ask where I wanted to go; since because of the dialect there I could not remember the name of the village and I believed that I could depend on what I had remembered of the roads. Finally it grew dark, and with no other choice I had to let the horse go where it wished, and that proved the best choice. The horse walked half the night through heath and woods; and, since I did not let it graze from the ground, it went home to its village; and I had to be resigned to my loss.

From this village the march went through Pomerania and Poland to Breslau. From Kalisch on we obtained wagons and were all driven in them to the camp near Frankenstein and Reichenbach. We arrived there in the month of June.

Before the fortress of Silberberg, all the regiments from Württemberg and also Bavarian soldiers had laid siege. The stronghold could not be stormed because of its height and would not surrender. The ground plan of this fortress could be examined by many of our men who were captured, but only after the war. During the war they were not allowed even to see the way they had to go.

After two weeks had passed, a few regiments remained before this fortress; and the others, in which I belonged, had to begin the siege at Glatz. When the blockade of this stronghold was begun, the Württemberg troops took up their camp in a rye field just blooming, and the straw was of the right length to serve for the barracks, which was a great advantage in camping.

When I arrived in this field, I hastened to look for my brother, who was in the Lilienberg Regiment. Here we met, embraced, and greeted one another, and joy filled our hearts. Then he took me to his barracks and gave me trousers, shirts, and several other pieces of clothing which I needed, since, as I have already said, I had lost almost everything at Colberg.

Then, when the stronghold of Glatz was surrounded by blockade,

MURAT, MARSHAL OF FRANCE AND KING OF NAPLES.

Murat played a significant role in the Russia Campaign, such as his success at Ostrovno. Unlike Ney who was renowned for his resilience during the withdrawal, described by Napoleon as the "bravest of the brave", Murat could not cope with the responsibility of his duty. He failed to hold Lithuania, and deserted the army to preserve his Kingdom of Naples.

several surprise attacks were undertaken against us, which always ended, nevertheless, in a loss to the Prussians. After two weeks had passed, we undertook against the town and the fortress an attack which started from each camp at about one o'clock at night. Everyone had to be careful to prevent any noise from the rifles and cannon, and we moved in columns through the grain fields toward the outposts. The men were already wet through up to their necks from the dew on the grain. Then the outposts began to fire, the 'command to storm was given, and everyone had to go through a river, at times up to his arms in water. A breastwork facing us was mounted, and under a rain of large and small bullets the Prussians along with their women and children were stabbed and shot to death, and some were hurled alive, together with their horses and cannon, over the sides of the walls. Then the Lilienberg Regiment pressed upon the city gates, an attempt which, in spite of great losses, was of no avail, however. While the enemy had to defend themselves around and in the crowded part of the city, a terrible shelling of light and heavy artillery broke in upon us, and all of us had to abandon the positions we had taken. Large mines were exploded in the breastwork, and everywhere there flew rockets, so-called pitch-rings, which could be put out only with small boxes as they fell on the ground.

So everyone returned to the camp in the "finest" disorder, and at daybreak everyone began looking up his friends. With fear-pressed heart I searched for my brother; and, as he was also looking for me, we found each other unharmed. Anyone who understands brotherly love can certainly imagine our joy at this moment.

When this attack was over, it was said that we would attack again the next night if the fortress did not surrender. This attack was not made, however, because of the announcement of peace. If anyone would or could be an onlooker at frightful explosions, he could get the finest view at a fortress attack, which is a more remarkable sight by far than a battle on a field. The bombs and grenades criss-crossing in the air in such great numbers, all floating like balls of fire in the air and exploding or bursting in the air or on the ground with a small cannon report, the slow ascent of each shell, the fast descent, often also a collision of them in the air-all this is a sight of moving beauty. It is different with the rockets which fly invisibly by with a small whisper. The grenades, however, and more so the bombs, behave like vultures in the air which race past the ear with storming wings.

We remained a few days longer in the camp, then came to a permanent camp in the region near Reichenbach, and were finally stationed every two weeks in another region. On St. Jacob's Day all the Württembergers had to leave Silesia, go by way of Frankfort-on-the-Oder, and take up permanent camp in the Brandenburg district, especially the region around Berlin near Stargard, Fürstenwalde, Beeskow, etc.

Here we stayed for eleven weeks among these poor peasants, who because of the infertility of the region had no provisions except potatoes, beans, and mutton. In speaking often of the good food which they had to give us, they hinted that they believed we must come from good country, since we, having the best of food, did not show any appreciation of it and because of our appetite had butchered all their sheep.

For one who wishes to discuss the poverty and its causes, my observations are set forth in the following manner: First, these people still owe their noblemen too much socage service in that the baron demands a quartershare cottager's hired hand or son to work for him four, five, or six days weekly without wages. Likewise he takes a daughter for six years without paying her wages just as the reigning prince takes the son for his army. A half or full-share cottager has to serve more, in proportion to the size of his property; so there are still villages where a man with his wife and children must work from three to five days for the nobleman, the fourth, fifth, or only the sixth day remaining for him to work for himself. However, he gets as much land from the baron for himself as he wants, or is able to till.

Second, the soil is only light sand, so that when sown to seed the tilled patches must even be beaten with a lath and, to prevent the blowing away of sand and seed, must be pressed down firmly. Naturally, therefore, only oats, potatoes ("Undeln"), and rye, seldom any wheat, can be grown.

Third, there is a lack of culture, especially of physical training, of willingness to work, of understanding and religion. Seldom does anyone go to church, only old grandmothers and old men, so that often, as I saw myself, the preacher would read his Sunday sermon for eight or ten persons with a similar lack of ardor. I learned also from my landlord, who had a boy of eleven or twelve years of age, that this boy could not read or write and did not know religious teachings. A book lying there gave me occasion to find this out.

French Headquarters, Willenberg, Prussia, June 10th 1812.

As I was reading, I happened to run across the Ten Commandments. I asked whether the Ten Commandments were taught to the children in the schools. The landlord said, "Yes, they are supposed to be taught, but my son does not know them yet, nor can he read or write. I must demand, however, that he still be taught it." Since, therefore, these people are little educated even in their own religion, un-Christian and heretical books serve to make them hate other denominations, and such people are weak enough to believe fables of this kind. I became convinced of this as I read in such a book and afterward spoke of it to the landlord. Therefore I played the part of a gravedigger, bound a stone to this book, and sank it in the big lake.

After I had been in this village for three months, the entire corps journeyed home. The march went through Plauen, Nuremberg, Bayreuth, Ansbach, and Dinkelsbühl, into Ellwangen. The King awaited us and then reviewed us there on the Schlossfeld. It was extraordinarily cold on this day, although we did not consider this unusual, since we were already accustomed to cold. Before we came to Ellwangen, my company passed the night in the little town of Weiltingen, which is "Old Württembergian." There everyone was supposed to give shouts of joy at crossing the border, but this was followed by a good deal of swearing because of the bad quarters we were given there. This campaign was now ended, and my two sisters and friends visited us two brothers. The reunion was a joy which could not have been greater evidence of family love.

CHAPTER II

*While I was working in various ways at my trade after the
Prussian campaign, the war with Austria broke out in
1809, and I was called into the garrison at Stuttgart. My
regiment and several others were already on the march to
Schorndorf, and the route was to lead through Bavaria.
On the way, however, a courier overtook us, bringing the
command to march back to Stuttgart again the next day,
and then we struck a route toward Tyrol through the
Adlerberg territory. We came then through Hechingen,
through the Killerthal, Saulgau, Altshausen, and then the
Monastery of Weingarten. There we were already meeting
outposts of the enemy, but we still had good quarters and
especially a lot of wine from the Lake [of Constance].*

When the Tyrolean insurgents heard of a large army reenforced by the
allied Baden and French forces, they retreated, and we moved forward on
all sides. The army then went through Ravensburg and to Hofen on the
Lake of Constance while the enemy moved with several skirmishes to
Lindau and finally back into the mountains.

In Hofen the Lilienberg Regiment was also stationed, in which my
brother served, and we met in his quarters. It is easy to imagine that we
two brothers rejoiced heartily at our reunion. The worry of one of us about
the possible misfortune of the other was so much greater because we
could seldom see and never protect each other.

Marshal Michel Ney, Duke of Elchingen, Prince of Moscow

After the aforesaid reunion I had to go through Buchhorn to Lindau. This latter city lies on an island in the lake, and a wooden bridge leads into it. The insurgents had to move out of this city for fear of being shut in. The first battalion of my regiment stayed ten weeks in this city, in which French horsemen were also stationed. During this time we had to make frequent attacks upon the enemy, among which the following were especially noteworthy.

As I stood at my outpost with the picket near the bleaching meadow facing Bregenz, the enemy moved in over the vineyards. The outposts had to move back to the picket. The picket fired, but the enemy approached. While each soldier fired wherever he could take a position, everyone stationed himself behind the bleaching house and took up the defense. To be able to aim better, I ran into a bleaching hut built of boards which lay well forward. A staircase went up from the outside, and I stationed myself on this, resting my rifle on the railing, where I could take aim at every man who approached. During the time while I was firing forty out of my sixty cartridges, the bullets kept raining down like hail upon my hut, and the enemy came too close upon me. Now I sprang down the steps and across the meadows back to the picket, which, however, was already retreating toward the city. Then I had to jump through gardens and hedges, and the enemy came to the gate just a little later than I did. I almost choked, gasping for breath.

When all of us had retreated into the city, the enemy remained outside the city three days, firing continually. We, however, had erected a bridge-head (breastwork) of sandbags and a trench and defensive iron spikes. We fired through the loopholes and from the wall with cannon and small guns. During the heavy shelling I shot a man in front of a garden house as he came a little way forward toward the breastwork and aimed into the loophole; but, after I shot and he suddenly fell, several others wanted to carry off this dead man, as was often done; however, the more openly it was done, the more often other men were hit too. Finally we fired with cannon, throwing projectiles into the large and beautiful garden houses, setting them all in flames. On the third day the enemy could no longer hold out, because of the heavy artillery fire, and moved back into the mountains.

Camp of the Italian Guard Dragoons, Willenberg area, Prussia, June 10th 1812.

As soon as the road was cleared, the trees standing in the gardens were cut down by the thousands, along with the beautiful box hedges which stood there tall and beautiful like walls, and the rest of the buildings were completely torn down, so that they would not be a hindrance to the shelling any more. This inflicted a damage of one million florins on the city.

After a time we again undertook a general attack, for which the Lilienberg Regiment, Baden and French soldiers, and the sharpshooters joined us. The enemy was attacked in front of Lindau and was driven in retreat back into the mountains. Before the attack volunteers were called upon to advance by skirmishes, and I went with them. The number was 160 men in all, and we were under the command of a lieutenant. Under the continual firing about fifty sharpshooters were cut off from us during the pursuit and led captive into the mountains. All of us volunteers pressed halfway up the mountain which was two hours distant from Lindau in order to recover the captives. When we saw that the columns advancing behind us were no longer following but were dividing in the middle and that our detachment had moved three quarters of an hour too far away, we heard the firing far to the left and far to the right as though it came from Kempten and, to the right, from Bregenz. This seemed to be a turning of our men into retreat, which assumption proved to be true. Now the lieutenant wanted to retreat with us, but we all complained at that and still wanted to bring back the captives from the mountains. The lieutenant would not give in, and we had to go back to a little village at the foot of the mountains. When we came into this village, we were fired upon from the houses and gardens and our army had already retreated halfway toward Lindau. Everyone then had to rely upon his legs; and, amid much firing, we had to run until we almost choked for want of air. We met the whole corps in an oak wood a half hour out of Lindau. Here we wanted to

In ferocious fighting, Austrian grenadiers attempt to storm the fortified granary in the village of Essling during the campaign of 1809 on the Danube.

take a stand, but could not because of the danger of being surrounded by insurgents.

Now the detachment retreated slowly until near the city, and then took up again the position for firing. Here we held out for half an hour, everyone firing as much as he could. The cannon were hauled out, but the grapeshot fire did not help either, since the enemy formed a halfmoon line and only a few could be hit, for they lay down on the ground behind the hedges, trees, and hills, while every shot of theirs could hit our compressed column. Finally too many of our men fell, and the enemy drew near the city gate in order to cut everyone off; this hurried our retreat into the city.

Noteworthy was the state of the peasants who had to drive the wagons to pick, up the wounded and who had to come right along at the time of

French headquarters, Sensbourg, Eastern Prussia, June 13th 1812

the attack. Four men and four horses were hitched to each wagon. As soon as the firing began, they had to stay with us. From then on, none of them could be seen sitting upright on his horse: they were all lying down on their horses, and those on the wagons flung themselves down amidst a fearful howling. In addition, they were given blows because of their fear.

During this time that I was at Lindau, the second battalion of the Franquemont Regiment, which was stationed at Wangen and Isny, was made completely captive. Later peace was made, and we marched into Bregenz, a town up on the Lake of Con stance. However, the entrance into this city was looked upon as a somewhat hostile move. For the sake of security several regiments coming from the mountains entered it from behind, and those from Lindau moved in from the front.

Indeed, the Regiment of Lilienberg had once before been forced to flee after a conquest of the town. It happened in this way: while the soldiers were looking about for booty in the cellars and houses, the enemy moved into the town and drove everyone out through the narrow pass in the mountain, which has three outlets. On this occasion the enemy should have pressed their advantage. Rather than rushing dispersed into the attack, they might better have occupied the three outlets and made captives of everyone. Instead, they only fired down from the mountains at their fleeing enemies in the pass, not having occupied the outlets strongly enough.

When our before-mentioned entry into Bregenz began, there was once more disorder among the soldiery. Cellars were broken into, and wine was carried out in buckets everywhere. Even several kegs were left running. Everyone became intoxicated until finally a strict order put an end to all this. We drank especially a great deal of very thick red Tyrolean wine, and we had everything in abundance. When, however, a new day arrived and all had moved into their quarters, everything became quiet, and the property of the citizens was safeguarded.

I stayed there almost three weeks at the home of a chimney sweep, together with nine other men, and we had everything, in particular as much as we could drink, wine and cherry brandy. After three weeks my regiment was moved to Dornbirn, which was a large marketing center lying in the Rhine Valley between Switzerland and Tyrol. In this town I came into the house of a furrier, who himself was still with the insurgents. His wife had a little child about three-quarters of a year old. This child was remarkably beautiful, and I, too, had my fun with it.

Once I gave this child some brandy to drink. Little by little the child took a liking to it, so that it became a bit intoxicated and so gleeful that I had to keep it from falling down from the pillow; this was great fun and did not do the child any harm. I stayed another period of about three weeks in these quarters, and in the entire village the people were quite friendly.

The householders in this village and the surrounding region have several maids who come from the Tyrolean Alps. These maids are especially remarkable for their dress. All their black skirts are of one piece with the bodice and have a great number of pleats all around. Upon their heads they wear large black caps, which likewise have curious pleats and are large and round like beehives in form. These maids have especially pretty and rosy-colored faces, which is said to come from eating milk and cheese. As to sociability, however, there is not much to say for them, since they are shy and not very talkative. They showed this even more toward orderly soldiers, as I know from experience, since there were two such maids in my house. It often happened, when they were sitting at their meal

French headquarters, Rastenburg, Eastern Prussia, June 14th 1812.

and I would joke with them decently, that they would jump up from the table and run out of the room, and then it was difficult to get them to come back again.

Regarding the fertility of this region, there is not much rye or German wheat, so much the more corn, however. The bread in particular is usually of nothing but corn. When you look at the bread, you believe that it is made of the finest kernels. When eating it, however, you notice it is coarse, heavy, and soggy. Wood is not cheap either; and in place of it in the entire Rhine Valley they dig peat, that is, sod which is a grayish red. This is cut and piled up, dried in the air and sun, and then burned in stoves instead of wood.

During this time, from spring to fall, we always had the great snow-capped mountains before, and later around us. Every time that it had rained, even in the greatest heat in August, one could see that the mountains were covered with new snow to a third of the distance down from the top.

In the month of October, we again marched homeward, and the route led through Wangen, Ravensburg, Altdorf, and Waldsee, and from there to Biberach, where we all had to stay for some time, being quartered in the surrounding villages. I also was assigned to a village and to the house of a well-to-do peasant who had a sister, a nun who was living at home. Since I would read books frequently on certain days and the nun noticed my behavior, she asked me why I always read and was so thoughtful. I said that my former circumstances gave me occasion to do that.

Since I kept trying to be pleasant to her and was able to draw her attention-more and more toward me, she asked others about my situation. Now I thought that since this thing had been started it must be carried on. I spoke to all my comrades located in the village, saying that they should call me at times "Miller," at other times "Walter," and again "Kapuziner."

This was done. Then the nun said to me, "Now I know, indeed, where your devout reading comes from. You may as well confess it to me." So then I did her the favor and told her that my brother had been a priest and I a Capuchin monk, that I had already vowed my chastity, and also that my name had been Miller instead of Walter, which the malicious soldiers always applied to me. I finally told her that she had evidence here in my beard which I still wore on my chin.

From now on, these pious hosts were very sympathetic toward me, and the nun told me her entire cloister story, and they had a liking for me above all other soldiers, so much so that the old father wept tears. Especially when I left, he wept with the others, begging that if I loved them I should inform them of my future fate in distant . places. They even wanted to accompany me for several hours.

After the years 1810 and 1811 had passed by and I was, in 1811, at the house of my godfather, Master Craftsman Häfele, the innkeeper at Ellwangen, war once more broke out.

Légion polonaise, 1810.
RÉGIMENT DE LA VISTULE.

Soldiers from Napoleon's Polish Legion, Vistula regiment, 1810

CHAPTER III

In the month of January, 1812, I was recalled to the garrison of Schorndorf. From here the line of march went through Calw, Wüstenroth, and Oehringen. In the villages about Oehringen the regiments remained four or five days until the inspection was completed in Oehringen. From here the entire corps marched through Künzelsau, Mergentheim, Weikersheim, and through the Würzburg district, where it was generally rumored that we were going to Spain and would embark on the Baltic Sea. Although the outlook did not seem good, I and all the soldiers were very merry, always singing and dancing, especially since throughout the entire Würzburg country the quarters and eating and drinking were very good, particularly because of the large supply of wine, so that everyone had his field flask voluntarily filled with wine and his pockets with cookies at the time of departure. Moreover, the beautiful villages on the Main River, surrounded by vineyards, fruit trees, and grain fields, put everyone in a happy mood.

About the middle of March, the army continued on its way through Saxe-Coburg, where a wooded and mountainous region began; the pine trees were especially plentiful. In these mountains we came upon a valley which led out of the Thuringian Forest. In this valley there were sawmills every two or three hundred paces, and between them were little hamlets.

NAPOLEON ON HIS IMPERIAL THRONE, 1806
Jean Auguste Dominique Ingres (1780–1867)

When the valley turned to the right and our march to the left, as it went through the Thuringian Forest itself to Saxe-Weimar, we had to climb high as if up a roof. In this huge forest, snow still lay two feet deep, though during the whole march no more was to be seen. In the middle of the forest was a game park which was tightly enclosed with planks to a height of twelve feet and which was about an hour's walk long. The city where we afterward spent the night lay about an hour's walk away in the valley. From Weimar we turned somewhat to the left, continued through a few cities toward Leipsic, and in April entered Leipsic.

In the city of Leipsic anyone could see what was going to happen, since as many "Frenchies" as could slip through came crowding through the gates. Leipsic was packed with soldiers, and I was in quarters with 150 men; yet the landlord to whom we were assigned put us all in one

Italian Guards of Honour, Kalvary, June 24th 1812

Italian Guards of Honour, Marienpol, June 26th 1812

building, the former theater building, which was a hall 100 feet long and 60 feet wide. Triple rows of tables stood ready in the hall, very beautifully set and loaded with beer, brandy, butter, cheese, and white bread. After all had sat down, everybody ate and drank while eight servants brought in the warm meal, which consisted of white soup, two kinds of meat, and several kinds of vegetables. In addition, something cold was served for dessert, and drinks were served in abundance throughout the whole afternoon. We stayed here two days until the line of march formed by columns and the departure was ordered.

After leaving Leipsic, we found the quarters somewhat worse on account of the huge army of soldiers, and the march turned toward Torgau.

PRINCE JÓZEF PONIATOWSKI.
Josef Maria Grassi (1757–1838)

I had been in Torgau in 1807. In the meantime the city had built new fortifications. About the city, which it took an hour to walk around, there had been added two moats and besides four buttressed walls of nothing but beautifully hewn stones which had been shipped down the Elbe from Bohemia. These new huge walls especially attracted my attention, since I could examine them as a mason and a stonecutter; and so I saw that each of them was ten feet thick and that buttresses were set into the ground every ten feet behind them, each of them in turn ten feet thick and ten feet long. I noticed especially the beautiful jointing of the stones, most of which were ten feet long and three feet square and had been laid over the wall lengthwise. On the other side of the Elbe there were also casements facing eastward, which were all, even the roofwork, built of beautifully hewn stone.

And then we went farther and came to Fürstenwalde, a middle-sized city in the Brandenburg district. It was the region where my regiment had lain in fixed quarters for eleven weeks in 1807, and so many of us went to see our former landlords; several women also found their once beloved soldiers, although several men were hiding for good reason and did not wish to be found for fear they would be called a father. In this city I was quartered with a beer brewer. We stayed there several days. The opportunity was also taken to invite soldiers to communion, for which four Catholic and four Lutheran clergymen had been sent along with the corps from home. The church was Lutheran, but we held the Catholic services there, too; so I received communion. We were still very lively in this town, singing and living cheerfully, although we could imagine the unusual campaign before us; but everyone always believes in, and hopes for, the best. I also looked after my saber and made it very sharp at a turner's and tempered it in fire so that it would not break off. I saw in the eastern suburb of this little town a house, the timber framing of which was filled with bones cross-wise; instead of being walled in, these bones had moss between them. In general, the types of buildings in this region are of a poor appearance and quality so that a like condition may be assumed about the farming. From there the line of march turned toward Frankfort-on-the-Oder, where a halt was made. Here we were quartered for three days, and by this time we had to be contented with poor food and army bread. We had to drill even on Ascension Day; so General Hugel tried to remind his royal highness, the Crown Prince, not to drill, saying that it was a holiday. The Crown Prince, however, gave this answer: "I will do you a favor, General, and not arrest you. Do you think I don't know what day it is?" This indignant mood of our Crown Prince might well have been caused by the transfer of the Wurttemberg corps to General Ney, since the day before Ney had attached us to his 25th division and the 3rd army corps; and our Crown Prince, feeling his honor injured, was, therefore, angry with us.

From Frankfort the march was continued to Poland through the village of Reppen, where the use of the German language stopped, and the manners and culture made a strange impression. It was the month of May, and the air swarmed with May bugs so amazingly that it was hard to keep' your eyes open in the evening. The bugs were so very thick that they darkened the atmosphere, and everyone was busy shaking them out of his face and hair. Here it became necessary for each person to seek and cook his own provisions, although requisitioning was forbidden. However, everyone still had his full strength, and courage was still alive in every soldier. But from day to day privation and hunger increased, and it became necessary for the regiment to requisition and slaughter livestock so that the men could have some meat in addition to the potatoes and grits which they found here and there. Bread was rare, and there was nothing at hand to buy.

Italian Guards of Honour on the march, Michalsky, June 27th, 1812

Now we came to a Polish government town, Posen, to which I had brought the horses, wagons, and servants of a Polish general, as I noted in connection with the campaign of 1807. From there we went to Gnesen, also an important city, where I, likewise in 1807, had announced in eight villages that food must be delivered for Napoleon and where I had had to spend almost two weeks. In these towns it was still possible to buy provisions here and there, and supposedly quarters were still available there. The march continued through [Inowr]azlav, also a city where I had been during the Prussian campaigns, and all the roads of this district were still well known to me.

On Corpus Christi Day we marched into the city of Thorn, which lies on the northern bank of the Vistula River, another city in which I had been during the year of 1807. Here for the first time we saw all the corps

MARSHAL MICHEL NEY.
Known as "The Bravest of the Brave", and
arguably Napoleon's greatest marshal, Ney
displayed great courage in action, above
all during the retreat from Moscow, when
he was reputed to have been the last
Frenchman to leave Russian soil.

streaming together. All the gates were jammed, and the regiments had to wind through the streets in a great throng. We still obtained quarters. However, we had to prepare our own food from our rationed meat and bread. The meat came from the salted ice pits; there was a rumor that it had been stored from the war of 1807 - the condition of the meat made the rumor seem credible, since the meat appeared bluish-black and was salty as herrings. It was already tender enough to eat, and we boiled it a few times only to draw off the muriatic acid; and then the broth, not being useful for soup, had to be thrown out.

Since we stayed in Thorn on Corpus Christi Day, I attended the service in the great City Church, where I heard what was to me a very unusual sermon, because it was given in Polish and I could not understand anything of it. I also climbed the high, broad tower, which had more than a hundred steps, and saw the eight bells. The largest bell had a clapper that was taller than I was. An equally large clapper leaned against the wall, and I could not pull it by its upper part from the wall. This city had been improved as a fortress since my visit in 1807. The near-by heights were dug away, and ramparts were built, although with only wooden beams filled in between with sand instead of massive walls.

Now the orders led us from Thorn to Mariampol. The march there went through Seeburg, Bischofstein, and Lagarben. The roads were sandy, and dust covered our clothing. Thence we went to a village called Löventin, where we saw a strange sight: we could count as many as thirty stork nests; almost all the storks had nested in tall willow trees and stalked around the swamps in flocks like the geese at home. The route led us on through Nordenburg and Darkehmen. Then we came to a little town known as Kalvaria, which lay on a dead-level in a barren region. Here only a noon halt was made, and no one had anything to eat. Since all is allowed to necessity, this little town, although already plundered, could not remain unsearched. All the soldiers ran for food and water, and it so happened that what provisions the inhabitants had hidden were found and brought into the camp, even though it was Polish country and, therefore, friendly. Because of this fact, the inhabitants of the town complained to our Crown Prince; and, therefore, the command came that the first soldier who thus left camp would be shot. I returned to the camp, however, just in time. The determination of our Crown Prince had risen so high that he rode along the front with a pistol and held it on the breasts of some soldiers so that one might have almost believed some of them were

PRINCE PYOTR IVANOVICH BAGRATION

going to be shot, but their dire need with nothing to eat may have stopped him.

Daily the hardships increased, and there was no hope of bread. My colonel spoke to us once and said that we could hope for no more bread until we crossed the enemy border. The most anyone might still get was a little lean beef, and hunger made it necessary to dig up the fields for the potatoes already sprouting, which were, however, very sweet and almost inedible. One also heard everywhere that several men had already shot themselves because of hardship: in particular, an officer had cut his throat on that very same day. Finally we came to the Memel River, where the Russian border was. The town of Poniemon was located there. Everyone rejoiced to see the Russian boundary at last. We encamped at the foot of

Supply issues, Pilony area, by the Niemen river, Russia, June 29th 1812

the hill this side of the river, and everyone thought that he should make his knapsack as light as possible. I, too, searched through my pieces of clothing and threw away vests, unnecessary cleaning articles, trousers, etc. Here we had to make a halt until the pontoons were brought up and several bridges were constructed across the water. Now we believed that the Russians would wait on the other bank and attack, but nothing happened. Bonaparte fired upon the high points held by the Russians with a few cannon and sent his cavalry across the water. The Russians, however, withdrew after a short encounter.

On June 25 the army went over the bridges. We now believed that, once in Russia, we need do nothing but forage - which, however, proved to be an illusion. The town of Poniemon was already stripped before we could enter, and so were all the villages. Here and there a hog ran around and then was beaten with clubs, chopped with sabers, and stabbed with bayonets; and, often still living, it would be cut and torn to pieces. Several times I succeeded in cutting off something; but I had to chew it and eat it uncooked, since my hunger could not wait for a chance to boil the meat. The worst torture was the march, because the closed ranks forced all to go in columns; the heat and the dust flared up into our eyes as if from smoking coal heaps. The hardship was doubled by the continual halting of the troops whenever we came to a swamp or a narrow road. Often one had to stand for half an hour; then another such period was spent catching up and drudging away without water or food.

The march proceeded day and night toward Vilkomirz and Eve. Meanwhile it rained ceaselessly for several days, and the rain was cold. It was all the more disagreeable because nothing could be dried. Bodily warmth was our only salvation from freezing to death. I had on only one pair of blue linen trousers, which I had bought at Thorn, since I had thrown away my underwear because of the former heat. Thus I was constantly wet for two days and two nights, so that not a spot on my body was dry. Nevertheless, I did not remain behind although I could not see the way at night and slid in ever; dIrectIOn on account of the clay soil. Indeed, the soldiers fell about me so incessantly that most of them were completely covered with mud and some were left lying behind.

During the third night a halt was made in a field which was trampled into a swamp. Here we were ordered to camp and to make fires, since neither village nor forest could be seen and the rain continued without end. You can imagine in what a half-numbed condition everyone stood here. What could we do? There was nothing that we could do but stack the rifles in pyramids and keep moving In order not to freeze. Finally an estate was found off to one side, and all the soldiers by groups immediately ran to build a shelter. There was nothing else to do except to use all our strength and to pull out poles and straw. so I with assistance built a little shelter, but my strength did not last long enough to collect firewood. I lay in the tent shelter, hungry and wet. The comrades, however, who came in and lay down upon me served as a warm cover.

When dawn came, I hurried again to the manor. Meanwhile a cellar full of brandy had been discovered. I, too, pushed myself into the cellar and filled my field flask. I returned to the shelter with this and drank it without even any bread. Then by noon I noticed that half the men had stayed back and several had suffocated in the swamp. The brandy helped, but many a man drank himself to death because he would become numbed and would freeze on account of the wet and cold. My drummer, by the name of Schafer, met such an end.

In the evening, when some cow's meat was distributed, with difficulty we started a fire, so that meat and broth soon warmed our stomachs. Then the march continued toward the little town of Maliaty, where a two-day halt was made and the sick were taken to the hospital. In this bivouac we

The Viceroy's headquarters at Pilony, June 30th 1812

obtained some meat; but most of the men could no longer digest the pure meat, diarrhea seized many, and they had to be abandoned. In this camp I took the opportunity to wash my shirt and trousers. It happened to be good weather; but, in order to obtain water for drinking and cooking, holes were dug into the swamps three feet deep in which the water collected. The water was very warm, however, and was reddish-brown with millions of little red worms so that it had to be bound in linen and sucked through with the mouth. This was, of course, a hard necessity on our nature and ways.

Then we had to march farther through the villages of Kosatschisna [?], Labonary, Diescony [?], Drysviaty, Braslav, toward Disna, where we arrived in the middle of July. The men were growing weaker and weaker every day and the companies smaller and smaller. The march was kept up

Delzon's 13th and Broussier's 14th Divisions cross the Niemen River

day and night. One man after another stretched himself half-dead upon the ground; most of them died a few hours later; several, however, suddenly fell to the ground dead. The chief cause of this was thirst, for in most districts there was no water fit for drinking, so that the men had to drink out of ditches in which were lying dead horses and dead men. I often marched away from the columns for several hours in search of water, but seldom could I return with any water and had to go thirsty. All the towns not only were completely stripped but were also half-burned.

Finally we arrived at Polotsk, a large city on the other side of the Dvina River. In this region I once left the bivouac to seek provisions. There were eight of us, and we came to a very distant village. Here we searched all the houses. There were no peasants left. I later realized how heedless I had been, since each one ran into a house alone, broke open everything that was covered, and searched all the floors and still nothing was found.

Finally, when we assembled and were ready to leave, I once more inspected a little hut somewhat removed from the village. Around it from top to bottom were heaped bundles of hemp and shives, which I tore down; and, as I worked my way to the ground, sacks full of flour appeared. Now I joyfully called all my comrades so that we might dispose of the booty. In the village we saw sieves; these we took to sift the flour mixed with chaff an inch long; and, after that, we refilled the sacks.

Then the question of carrying and dividing the grain arose, but it occurred to me that I had seen a horse in one of the houses. Everyone immediately hurried to find the horse. We found two instead of one, but unfortunately they were both colts, and one could not be used at all. We took the largest, placed two sacks on it, and started out very slowly. While we were marching there, the Russians saw us from a distance with this booty; and at the same moment we saw a troop of peasants in the valley, about fifty. These ran toward us. What could we do but shoot at them? I, however, led the horse, and a second man held the sacks while the rest fired, one after another, so that the peasants divided in order not to be hit so easily; but they could not take the sacks away from us.

We hurried toward the bivouac, but on the way we found a deep stream of water, and only a round tree trunk lay across it. Now the question arose how to take the horse and sacks across. I said, "Why, I will carry the sacks across, and we will throw the horse into the water," and, indeed, I succeeded in getting over the narrow bridge in an upright position without the use of handrails, which feat might have cost me my life, since the river was very deep. Then the horse was thrown in and driven across with stones, the sacks were then reloaded, and we finally marched into bivouac. That was a joy! Whatever each person could not use was distributed. Then dough was made, and little balls were molded with the hands and baked, or rather roasted, in the fire. This food lasted me a week, and I thanked

God for the chance gift which had remained buried under the shives until I came.

We then marched farther in a somewhat more eastern direction through Ula, Beshenkovichi, and Ostrovno, and near the end of July toward Vitebsk. Often on the way to Vitebsk we undertook a raiding excursion. Some thirty of our men went off the main route to find a still inhabited and unstripped village. We collected our strength and walked from three to four hours in hopes of rejoining the army at the second bivouac.

We were fortunate and found a village where everything still seemed to be in order. To safeguard our small group, we left a rear-guard behind and agreed that they should report with certain shooting signals a possible attack from the Russians. As we entered the village, a man at once approached us who was probably sent as an interpreter from the mayor to learn our desires. We told him that we required provisions for the army - if we received them voluntarily, force would not be used. He reported it to the village, but the answer was of no good; so we were compelled two by two to take a house and search it. I joined forces with a comrade but found nothing except milk and cabbage "Kapuke").

A wooden hut stood on a farm. This was locked, and the peasants would not open it. When we broke down the door, a woman who was with child came running at us as if mad and wanted to throw us out, but we forced her back with gentle thrusts. Here we obtained some flour, eggs, and fat. When all brought their findings together later, our booty was considerable. I am telling of this undertaking to show the ways of the Russian subjects. If they had voluntarily removed the simple covers (of their storage places), much of the household furniture would have remained unspoiled, for it was necessary to raise the floors and the beams in order to find anything and to turn upside down everything that was covered. Under one such floor, which had large beams resting side by

Headquarters, Kroni, 1st July 1812

side, we found pots full of sausages stuffed into casings four to five feet long and filled with pieces of bacon and meat an inch thick. Although such sausages already had a fierce smell, they were quickly eaten. Here were also hidden pots filled with lumps of cheese, which according to the customs of the country had been placed as milk on the fire and had been allowed to curdle so that the milk, cheese, and fat floated about in chunks. The cheese and fat were still left for us.

In another well-plundered village nothing could be found in the houses; and so, urged on by our hunger, we dug in the ground. Here I with several others removed a large pile of wood which had probably just been put there. We removed this, dug into the ground, and found a covered roof of planks. There was an opening under this from ten to twelve feet deep. Inside there were honey jars and wheat covered with straw. When we had all this, we opened the jars and saw a solid, white substance with the appearance of hard wax. It was so hard that one had trouble breaking off a piece with his saber; but, as soon as it was put on the fire, it all melted to very dear honey. Now I had honey to eat for a week, although without bread. I ate the wheat raw and wild calamus from the swamps; and, in general, what garden roots were to be found had to serve the most extreme hunger.

After this raiding excursion we again met the corps in bivouac; and we came then, on August 16, toward the city of Smolensk. Here my company had only 25 fit men. At Vitebsk already regiments had been formed into a few battalions, and many officers were left without duties, among them was my captain, whose name was Arrant. Here everyone had to be prepared for battle. The city lay before us on a long ascending height, and on the other side was the Dnieper River. Even on the night of our arrival there were a few skirmishes with the outposts and vanguard.

On the morning of August 17, every regiment was set in motion, and all advanced in columns against the Russians. Here every regiment without exception was under fire. Again and again the troops attempted assaults, but because of the greater number of the Russians we were forced back every time on this day, since their heavy artillery stood on the heights and could hit everything.

Finally by night we had made good our position on the heights overlooking the city, and the battle was discontinued. In the course of these events hunger could no longer be thought of. During the night, however, I ate from my little bit of honey and raw supplies without being able to cook. The thought of the coming day alternated with fitful sleep, and in fantasy the many dead men and horses came as a world of spirits before the last judgment. Since I did not suffer the misfortune of being ·wounded, I thought: "God, Thou hast allowed me to live till now. I thank

Thee and offer up my sufferings to Thee and pray Thee at the same time to take me further into Thy protection."

This and several other pious meditations I had with God, and I considered my destiny. Although it was never quiet the entire night and though a new battle might have started at any hour, none of all my miseries was so hard and depressing as the thought of my brothers, sisters, and friends. This thought was my greatest pain, which I sought to repress with this hope: "With God everything is possible; so I will depend upon

The Viceroy having a nap, Riconti, Vilna area, July 3rd 1812.

His further help."

As soon as the day broke - here I cannot omit the description of the length of the day and the shortness of the night. Many times when we went into bivouac for the night, the great glow of the sun was still in the sky so that there was only a brief interval between the setting and the rising sun. The redness remained very bright until sunrise. On waking one believed that it was just getting dark, but instead it became bright daylight. The nighttime lasted three hours at most, with the glow of the sun continuing. So, as soon as the day broke-we marched against the city. The river was crossed below the city. The suburbs on the northern side were stormed, set on fire, and burned up. My company's doctor, named Stäuble, had his arm shot away in crossing the stream, and he died afterward. No longer could I pay any attention to my comrades and, therefore, knew not

The Imperial Guard, Vilna area, July 3rd 1812

in what way they perished or were lost. Everyone fired and struck at the enemy in wild madness, and no one could tell whether he was in front, in the middle, or behind the center of the army.

Finally, while cannon balls kept on raining out of the city, we stormed it. With the help of heavy cannon, most of the supporting piers on the high old city wall, on which the Russians were defending themselves from the inside, were partially destroyed. We broke through the gates, pressed from all sides against the city, and put the enemy to flight. When I entered the city, we went toward the cloisters and churches. I also hurried into the great church which stood to the right in the city on a hill facing the valley. I did not meet any of the enemy within, however. Only priests ("Bopen") were there praying. They had on long black cowls, ragged hose, and old slippers. The church was large and on the inside built round. It had many holy images and altars as ours do. The only difference was that there was no holy water. The church had five towers, one on each corner and one in the middle of the roof. On every tower were triple iron crosses, and from each cross went intervening chains from one tower to another; this created a beautiful appearance from without.

After the Russians had been stormed from the two suburbs, from which one road on the left leads to St. Petersburg and another on the right to Moscow, and after the wooden houses there lay in ruins, we resorted in the evening to the former camping ground. Here one saw the wounded men brought together to be operated on in a brick kiln which lay on the heights above the city. Many arms and legs were amputated and bandaged. It all looked just like a slaughter house. In the city itself over half of the buildings were burned; these included, especially in the upper part of the city, many large, massive houses which were burned out on the inside. Many roofs of sheet copper were rolled up and lay about. In one building west of the city I saw the lower story filled with paper, and on top it was burned black; probably all the official documents had been hurried to that place.

On August 19, the entire army moved forward, and pursued the Russians with all speed. Four or five hours' farther up the river another battle started, but the enemy did not hold out long, and the march now led to Moshaisk, the so-called "Holy Valley." From Smolensk to Moshaisk the war displayed its horrible work of destruction: all the roads, fields, and woods lay as though sown with people, horses, wagons, burned villages and cities; everything looked like the complete ruin of all that lived. In particular, we saw ten dead Russians to one of our men, although every day our numbers fell off considerably. In order to pass through woods, swamps, and narrow trails, trees which formed barriers in the woods had to be removed, and wagon barricades of the enemy had to be cleared away. In such numbers were the Russians lying around that it seemed as if they were all dead. The cities in the meantime were Dorogobush, Semlevo, Viasma, and Gshatsk. The march up to there, as far as it was a march, is indescribable and inconceivable for people who have not seen anything of it. The very great heat, the dust which was like a thick fog, the closed line of march in columns, and the putrid water from holes filled with dead people, and cattle brought everyone close to death; and eye pains, fatigue, thirst, and hunger tormented everybody. God! how often I remembered the bread and beer which I had enjoyed at home with such an indifferent pleasure! Now, however, I must struggle, half wild, with the dead and living. How gladly would I renounce for my whole life the warm food so common at home if I only did not lack good bread and beer now! I would not wish for more all my life. But these were empty, helpless thoughts. Yes, the thought of my brothers and sisters so far away added to my pain! Wherever I looked, I saw the soldiers with dead, half-desperate faces. Many cried out in despair, "If only my mother had not borne me!"

Headquarters, Nev-Trokiy, July 4th 1812

Some demoralized men even cursed their parents and their birth.

These voices, however, raised my soul to God, and I often spoke in quietude, "God, Thou canst save me; but, if it is not Thy will, I hope that my sins will be forgiven because of my sufferings and pains and that my soul will ascend to Thee." With such thoughts I went on trustingly to meet my fate.

On September 7, every corps was assigned its place, and the signal to attack was given. Like thunderbolts the firing began both against and from the enemy. The earth was trembling because of the cannon fire, and the rain of cannon balls crossed confusedly. Several entrenchments were stormed and taken with terrible sacrifices, but the enemy did not move from their place. The French Guard, according to order, was placed behind the attacking corps to bring about the final decision. Now the two armies moved more vigorously against one another, and the death cries and shattering gunfire seemed a hell. Nine entrenchments were stormed, the French threatened to surround the enemy from the front, and finally the enemy gave way.

This beautiful grain region without woods and villages could now be compared to a cleared forest, a few trunks here and there looking gray and white [?]. Within a space an hour and a half long and wide, the ground was covered with people and animals. There were groans and whines on all sides. The stream separated the battlefield into two parts. On the left of the water stood a row of a few houses which looked as if transformed into a chapel for the dead. Over the river there was a wooden bridge that had been burned. On account of the congestion before and during the burning,

The courtyard of Holzany Castle, Viceroy of Italy's headquarters, July 11th 1812.

the banks on both sides of the bridge were filled with dead piled three and four deep. Particularly the wounded who could still move hurried to the river to quench their thirst or to wash their wounds; but the suffering brothers had no help, no hope of rescue: hunger, thirst, and fire were their death.

Although this terrible sight looked like a kingdom of the dead, the people had, nevertheless, become so indifferent to their feelings that they all ran numbly like shades of death away from the piteous crying. We moved forward and camped by a forest on a height facing Moscow; it was a wood of green trees. Here we not only had nothing to eat but also no water to drink, because of the high camp site; and the road through the fields was still covered with dead Russians. Now we traveled with somewhat higher hopes toward Moscow yet with the expectation that we should clash again with the Russians, but the Russians thought themselves too weak and went through the city setting fire to many parts, and the inhabitants were abandoned. Our troops came unexpectedly, something which the Russians before had believed impossible, because there never had been a foreign enemy who had reached and conquered the old city of the Tsar, the capital city. All the merchants and people of the city could not flee swiftly enough to save themselves, and many costly articles were left behind. Even though the French Guard occupied the city first and took possession of wine, bread, etc., for their army, there still remained a good deal for us, the allies. We marched in, too, and took quarters behind the Kremlin in the so-called German suburb, which ran from west to east behind the city proper.

On the march into the city or rather on the march toward it, from a hill in a forest an hour and a half away, we saw the huge city lying before us. Clouds of fire, red smoke, great gilded crosses of the church towers glittered, shimmered, and billowed up toward us from the city. This holy city was like the description of the city of Jerusalem, over which our Saviour wept; it even resembled the horror and the wasting according to the Gospel. Farther inward toward the city was a wide plain; and in front of the city ran the stream Alia, over which there was a wooden bridge. As we marched through, I observed as much as I could: there were broad streets, long straight alleys, tall buildings massively built of brick, church towers with burned roofs and half-melted bells, and copper roofs which had rolled from the buildings; everything was uninhabited and uninhabitable. After a few hours' walking we went past the palace (Kremlin). Here was the stream Kremlin in an open, walled canal which runs through the city. At the lower end of the palace a street led toward the right to a beautiful parade ground; and behind this was the German suburb, which the Württemberg corps occupied for three weeks.

Here one could find and buy provisions; for each soldier was now citizen, merchant, innkeeper, and baker of Moscow. Everyone tried to dress as much as possible with silks and materials of all colors. Only tailors were lacking; silks, muslins, and red Morocco leather were all abundant. Things to eat were not wanting either. Whoever could find nothing could buy something and vegetables in sufficient quantity stood in the fields. Particularly was there an abundance of beets, which were as round and large as bowling balls and fiery red throughout. There were masses of cabbage three and four times as large in size as cabbage heads that we would consider large. The district called Muscovy is more favored in agriculture and climate, and more civilized than the regions toward St. Petersburg and those through which we had come. It was still good weather, and one could sleep warm enough under a coat at night.

After we had been citizens of Moscow for four weeks, we lost our burgher rights again. Napoleon refused the peace treaty proposed to him, and the army which had advanced some thirty hours' farther on had to

General Pino's Division - the rearguard - on the march, July 16th 1812

retreat, because the Russian army stationed in Moldavia was approaching. Now it was October 17, and Napoleon held an army review and announced the departure for October 18, early in the morning at 3 o'clock, with the warning that whoever should delay one hour would fall into the hands of the enemies. All beer, brandy, etc., was abandoned and whatever was still intact was ordered to be burned. Napoleon himself had the Kremlin undermined and blown Up. The morning came, and each took his privilege of citizenship [Bürgerrecht] upon his shoulders and covered it with his coat cape of strong woolen cloth, and everybody had bread pouches of red Morocco leather since everything would be destroyed that day anyhow we would drink it up. We drank and also let others drink from it, but all of us said, "How will this turn out?"

In the morning Major von Schaumberg saw me and noticed that I was

Sleeping on the banks of the River Niemen, a Guard horse artillery officer and French infantrymen.

still alert and spirited. He addressed me, saying that I ought to stay with him and take care of him along with his attendant. I consented and took over a horse and his equipage. Then everyone packed up, and the enemy attacked us. The decision was soon to the advantage of the Russians, and all ran in a crowded retreat, the army moving toward Kaluga with the Cossacks in front of and beside us. The enemy army behind us shattered all the army corps, leaving each of us then without his commanding officer. Those who were too weak to carry their weapons or knapsacks threw them away, and all looked like a crowd of gypsies.

I and my fellow attendant traveled with the major as best we could. At one time my fellow attendant said, "Walter, you look all yellow in the face. You have the jaundice!" I became frightened at this and believed that my end would soon have to come, too, though I actually felt nothing.

Then we came to a second city, Borovsk. Here the city was immediately ablaze; and, in order for us to get through, soldiers had to be used to quench the flames. Camp was pitched by this city, and it became dark. One no sooner thought of resting than the Russians fell upon our army and cut off many as captives. Everything was in confusion, and during almost the whole night the throng had to retreat to Moshaisk, everyone running so as not to fall into the hands of the enemy. Because of these considerable losses, cannon, munition wagons, coaches, and baggage wagons by the hundreds had to be thrown into the water; and, where that was impossible, all wagons were burned, not one wheel being permitted to remain whole. The sutlers, even the cavalry, had to give up their horses so that these could be hitched to the cannon. The fighting, the shrieking, the firing of large and small guns, hunger and thirst, and all conceivable torments increased the never-ending confusion. Indeed, even the lice seemed at his side, all had an odd appearance as they set out; they filled, as far as it was possible, everything with sugar and the so-called Moscow tea in order to withstand the future misery. The sugar melted out of the merchant shops in the conflagration and, half-burnt, resembled a brownish gray glauber salt.

When we assembled in the morning, my company was 25 privates strong, and all companies were more or less of this size. The march went forth to the right from behind the eastern side of the city, and we moved past the city on the south. There were two bridges thrown across the river below us, and the smoke from the flames surged up behind us. Up on the heights past the bridge to the left of the road stood a cloister in which there was a flour storeroom where everyone fetched as much as he could carry. Beyond the bridge there was a cabbage patch where millions of cabbage heads were still standing: it pained me not to be able to take along even one of these heads, since I fully expected the utmost famine.

From Moscow the road led south through Malo Jaroslavetz toward Kaluga. Near Jaroslavetz in the evening the Russian Moldavian army, which had come from Turkey, met us. In this city I was ordered on guard at the headquarters of the general staff while the army encamped in front of the city. Here the inhumanity of the commanders began to mount: the remaining troops' weapons were inspected, and many who did not have their weapons fairly rust-free got 12 to 20 strokes with a club until they were near desperation. While I looked after my post, a comrade said to me that he had on a near-by wagon a little cask of wine brought along from Moscow and that to seek supremacy, for their number on both officers and privates was in the thousands.

In times when death was near, God sent me help again and again. After midnight, when we pitched camp again following the above-mentioned pursuit by the Russians, a little village stood a quarter of an hour off the highway, and I crept with my master and two horses into a stable that still had a roof. There I saw hanging on a cord behind a grate a smoked pig's head. As if received from the hand of God, I took it off from the cord with a prayer of thanks. I, my master, and my fellow servant ate it with unbelievable appetite, and we felt life come to us again. Then I always thought: "If even a few should get to German soil, it is possible that I with God's help might also reach there." In these days it snowed for the first time, and the snow remained. The cold arrived at the same time, too, and the freezing of the people multiplied the number of the dead. No one could walk fifty paces without seeing men stretched out half or completely dead. According to Napoleon's scheme we were to strike leftward toward Galicia. The Russian, however, hindered us and drove us past Vereia and Verina and to the right into our old, desolate highway.

Dokzice on fire, July 18th 1812

Finally we went over the battlefield at Moshaisk in the Holy Valley. Here one saw again in what numbers the dead lay. From the battle site on to this place the corpses were dragged from the highways, and entire hollows were filled with them. Gun barrels lay one on top of another in many piles from fifteen to twenty feet in height and in width where we bivouacked for the night.

Here God once more came to my help in a wondrous way. As I sought to fetch water in the night with my field flask, I came to a lake in which a hole had been chopped through the ice, and I drew my water with much effort because of the pressure of those standing around. On the way back, a round ball resembling a dead sheep was lying on the ground. I picked it up and in astonished joy unwrapped a rolled-up Crimean fur that reached from my head down to my feet besides having a peculiar collar which

A Russian prisoner of war, Kamen, July 21st 1812

could be clapped over my head. With my eyes turned to heaven I prayed again to God and gave thanks for the abundant mercy which I had received just when help was obviously most necessary.

I hurried to my major and had already put on the fur. He saw me and called out loudly, "Aye, God! What do you have on?" "A fur, Major, that I found just now. Now I've at least a covering." "Oh," he said, "I'll give you my fur. It's also a good one. If we get home, then you can have it back again, or I'll pay you enough for it." Thus I took his fur, which was also beautiful, having a green silk lining so that it could be worn right side out or inside out. The next morning everyone hurried on his flight, and no one wanted to be the last.

We now came to Gshatsk, and this town was already in flames. Here again many cannon were thrown into the water and part of them buried. The pressure was so frightful that I and my major lost each other. Now I had the second horse to myself, and we could not find each other again that day, nor even for another ten days.

Thus in the evening I rode apart from the army to find in the outlying district some straw for the horse and rye for myself. I was not alone, for over a strip ten hours' wide soldiers sought provisions because of their hunger; and, when there was nothing to be found, they could hunt up cabbage stalks here and there from under the snow, cut off some of the pulp from these, and let the core slowly thaw out in their mouths. Nevertheless, this time I had a second considerable piece of luck. I came to a village not yet burned where there were still sheaves of grain. I laid these before the horse and plucked off several heads of grain. I hulled them, laid the kernels mixed with chaff' into a hand grinder which had been left in a house, and, taking turns with several other soldiers, ground some flour. Then we laid the dough, which we rolled into only fist-sized little loaves, on a bed of coals. Although the outside of the loaves burned to charcoal, the bread inside could be eaten. I got as many as fifteen such balls.

For further supply, whenever I came upon sheaves of grain, I picked the heads, rubbed off the kernels, and ate them from my bread sack during the

French cuirassier in 1809.

course of the day. Several times I also found hempseed, which I likewise ate raw out of my pocket; and cooked hempseed was a delicacy for me because the grains burst open and produced an oily sauce; yet since I could not get salt for cooking, it did not have its full strength.

When this good night was half over, I laid four sheaves over my saddle and rode, to the head of the army as usual. Toward the next night, however, in order to make a fire again, I rode off the highway. Wading in the deep snow was too hard for my horse; so I took a peasant's sled, which had only two slabs of bark for boards, put a collar made from a sack around the horse's neck, and tied two ropes from there to the sled. As I drove on again the same night, I had to cross a river about sixty feet wide, over which only four or five poles lay. I, therefore, knew of no other means than to carry the sled over on the poles and to force the horse to

Skirmishing in and around Bezenkovitschi, July 21st 1812

The Bavarian cavalry crossing at the Dvina River, July 24th, 1812.

swim across. Accordingly I carried the emptied sled across successfully, although my feet went knee-deep into the water because the poles sank. I brought the horse, which could swim well, being of a Russian breed, to the sled again, and drove on. At this river I met a man by the name of Wittenhöfer, from my native village, who was already deathly weak. I let him ride. He died after a few days.

I continued, then, this sled-riding through the burned cities of Viasma, Semlevo, and Dorogobush without finding my master. Once, while I was eating some of my aforementioned bread, several Frenchmen saw me. These inhuman men surrounded me with the pretext of buying bread; and, when the word "bread" was mentioned, everyone bolted at me, so that I thought my death was near; but through an extraordinary chance there came along some Germans, whom I now called to my aid. They struck at my horse so that most of the Frenchmen fell back from me and then were entirely beaten off.

Among these Germans were two sergeants from my regiment called N. and N. After I was free, they took my bread and walked away. Not they, I could see now, but rather their hunger and my bread were both my redeemers and, at the same time, my robbers. Although I had already given them a loaf, they robbed me! But this, my dear readers, is to be judged otherwise than you think. There are stories in which people have murdered and eaten each other on account of hunger, but certainly this incident was still a long way from murder. Since starvation had risen to a high degree, why could not such a thing happen? And, besides that, much of the humanity of man had already vanished because of hunger. Indeed, I even heard at that time that several men had been murdered for the sake of bread. I myself could look cold bloodedly into the lamenting faces of the wounded, the freezing, and the burned, as I shall tell later, and think of other things.

We arrived at Smolensk on November 12, having made, from Moscow to that city, 26 days and nights of travel without pausing a day. If we traveled only twelve hours daily, then we had retreated 312 hours up to Smolensk.

When I arrived at Smolensk, it was raining rather heavily, and my sled could be pulled only with great effort. When I came toward the city, the crowd was so dense that for hours I could not penetrate into the column, for the guard [i.e., Imperial Guard} and the artillery with the help of the gendarmes knocked everyone out of the way, right and left. With effort I finally pressed through, holding my horse by the head, and accompanied by sword blows I passed over the bridge. In front of the city gate I and my regiment, now disorganized, moved to the right toward the city wall beside the Dnieper River. Here we settled down and had to camp for two days. As had been reported to us beforehand, we were to engage in battle with the enemy here and also to get bread and flour from the warehouses. Neither of the two reports, however, proved to be true. The distress mounted higher and higher, and horses were shot and eaten. Because I could not get even a piece of meat and my hunger became too violent, I took along the pot I carried, stationed myself beside a horse that was being shot, and caught up the blood from its breast. I set this blood on the fire, let it coagulate, and ate the lumps without salt.

While we tarried two days at Smolensk, the Russians advanced and awaited us at Minsk. Everyone hastily fled. Cannon were thrown into the water. The hospitals were nearly all left to the enemy; and, as was commonly rumored, the hospitals were set afire and burned with their inmates. This is more credible when one considers the treatment of the captured Russians; for, when we were victors over the Russians, whole columns' of captives were transported past us, and anyone who stayed behind because of weakness and fell back as far as the rear guard was shot in the neck so that his brain always crashed down beside him. Thus every fifty to a hundred paces I saw another who had been shot with his head still smoking. All this was done to make our passage safe, so that no robber corps could be formed behind us. Very few of the captives, however, were saved from starvation.

Now, as the march went on, I had to leave my sled behind and to lay my baggage on the horse, upon which I also mounted often during the day. The cold increased again that same day, and the road became as smooth as a mirror from the rain so that the horses fell down in great numbers and could not get up again. Since my horse was a native of the country, it had no horseshoes and could always help itself up again when it had fallen. It had even the good custom, whenever we went downhill, of sitting down on its rump, bracing its front feet forward, and sliding into the valley in

Napoleon reconnoitres the right bank of the Dvina River, July 24th 1812

The road from Bezenkovitschi to Ostrovno, July 25th 1812

this fashion without my dismounting. Other German horses, though, had shoes which were ground entirely smooth and for this reason could not keep themselves from slipping; nor could these irons be torn off, since no one had a tool for that.

Until now I had not seen my major again and believed nothing else than that he must be dead. I always cared for my horse by riding out at night where some ' village blazed brightly, in order to get some rye sheaves for the horse and rye grains for myself. I often could not get feed for four or five days, but my "Goniak" [trotter] was indifferent if only from time to time he could get some old straw from the camp or some thatch straw from a burned house, nor could I notice that he was getting thin. If I found some rest at night, I served as a crib for him. I always hung the, halter strap on my arm or foot so that I could notice any attempts to take him away. I laid myself squarely before his feet; and, when he had something to eat, he ground away with his teeth for a short time. When he had nothing, he sniffed and snorted all over me. Not once did his hoof touch me. At the most he pressed my fur coat a little. Unless you tied your horse to yourself, the horse was stolen immediately.

After leaving Smolensk, we arrived on November 16, amid a thousand kinds of danger at Krasnoë, where the Russians received us, having in the meantime circled around to our front. Here the French Guard, with the remaining armed forces that could still be brought together, took its position along the highway and kept up the firing against the enemy as well as possible. Although the enemy had to yield, any movements on our part drew vigorous firing upon us. Unfortunately, all the time the greatest misery fell upon the poor sick, who usually had to be thrown from the wagons just to keep us from losing horses and wagons entirely and who were left to freeze among the enemies, for whoever remained lying behind could not hope to be rescued.

Here I once heard my master speak (rather yell) close in front of me, whereupon I called, "Major, is it you?" He glanced at me and cried out for joy, "Oh, God, dear valet, is it you? Oh, now I am glad that I have you again. Oh, I am so happy that you are still alive." I also showed my joy over this reunion, for my master still had his old German chestnut, his horse from home, and his other attendant was also with him with a second horse. Now he asked me whether I still had part of his sugar loaf and coffee. Sadly I had to say that once when I lay down behind a battlement near a fire-razed village at night a group of Cuirassier Guards pressed upon me and tore away from me the sack with the sugar and coffee; and I almost failed to keep my horse. I gave in, therefore, and chose another place to lie down, and in occupying my second spot I found straw lying about, with which my horse could still his hunger. I myself lay down on a spot that was soft and not frozen. Before departing I thought I would see why it was so soft and warm under me, and I saw a dead man whose unfrozen belly had served as my good bed. "And I set out upon my journey again, Major, without being able to meet you again." The major then said, "That does not matter now. I am glad that you are here again."

General Ney, about whom no one knew anything anymore, was in charge of the rear guard. He fought his way through to us. However, his forces were half gone. The march had to go on; and the striking, clubbing, and skirmishing commenced so frightfully that the cry of murder echoed all about. The Cossacks advanced upon the army from all sides. We came toward Dubrovna, and the throng was so great that those on foot were usually beaten and cudgeled to the right and the left of the roadway at such narrow passages as marshes, rivers, and bridges here my major and I were pushed apart and lost each other again. It was not possible to recognize one another except by voice. Everyone was disguised in furs, rags, and pieces of cloth; they wore round hats and peasant caps on their heads, and many had priest's robes from the churches. It was like a world turned upside down. I had had enough of my helmet at the very beginning of the retreat. I put on a round hat, wrapped my head with silk and muslin cloths and my feet with thick woolen cloth. I had on two vests and over my doublet a thick and large Russian coat which I had taken from a Russian in exchange for my own at Smolensk on the trip into Russia; and over all this I wore my thick fur. I was so enwrapped that only my eyes had an opening out of which I could breathe. From time to time I had to break off from this opening the ice that would immediately form again from my breath.

At night in Dubrovna, when the enemy had given up their maneuvers, everyone settled down in and around the place. Every night, the fires for warming could be seen over a region four hours' long and wide, reddening the sky like red cloth. The burning villages at the side contributed most to this sight, and the shrieking, beating, and lamenting did not stop for a minute. Again and again people died, and sometimes froze to death; these were people who pressed toward the fire but were seldom permitted to get there; so they died away from the fire, and very often they were even converted into cushions in order that the living would not have to sit in the snow.

In every bivouac soldiers who looked like specters crept around at night. The color of their faces, their husky breathing, and their dull muttering were horribly evident; for wherever they went they remained hopeless; and no one allowed these shades of death to drag themselves to the fire. Usually six, eight, or ten of us had to combine to build a fire, since no other wood was to be had except rafter pieces from burned houses, or

Advance on Ostrovno, July 25th 1812

The Battle of Ostrovno. The 8th Hussars destroy the Russian position under Murat's guidance, July 25th 1812.

trees lying around, shattered wagons, etc., and without the cooperation of the men nothing could be accomplished. Neither did we dare to fall asleep at the fire all at the same time, because no one was safe from stealing and robbery.

As we came to Orscha, it was said that we would get shoes and bread from a magazine, also oats for the horses; but this was impossible. In spite of the guards stationed around the storehouses, none of the doors could be opened, since everyone hit and shoved each other in order to get close to a door. I hurried there at first to obtain oats, but that was impossible until the guards could no longer stand their ground and the doors were sprung open. Then I climbed through a window opening, took several sacks of oats with the help of my comrades, and brought them to the camp fire.

Immediately thereafter a soldier who also shared in my fire came' with two loaves of bread. Now everyone's heart beat with eagerness, and everyone sprang toward the bread store. When we arrived, no one could get inside anymore, and those within could not come out because of the pressure. What was to be done? Many weak soldiers lay on the floor and were trampled down, screaming frightfully. I made for a window opening again; tore out the shutter, the wooden grating, and the window; and got five of the loaves, though they were trampled and broken. This was since Moscow the second bit of bread, for which I thanked God anew with tears.

Now we were all happy by the fire, and with renewed spirits we resumed our journey toward whatever fate had in store for us. Always I set my mind to it and constantly made my way toward the front of the army rather than to the rear. Very often I had to go back because of the Cossacks roaming about; then I joined the front of the column again so as not to be cut off from behind.

Between Orscha and Kochanova I again rode off to the side of the army toward a village which stood in flames, in order to warm myself for a short time in the night and to seek for whatever was available. No sooner had I lain down than the Cossacks came and caught whomever of us they could get. My horse had a peculiar intelligence; for, as soon as shots were fired, it turned and ran of its own accord with all its strength. In the absence of danger, however, striking it often did no good when I wanted to ride fast. Thus it saved me by flight, and we headed toward the army again. Those on foot who had also made the side march were caught and plundered. The Frenchmen were usually struck down by the Russians and not pardoned. Those who were German could reckon on pardon with certainty because, as it was said, the Russian Emperor had commanded that the Germans be spared, since the Empress, as is known, was a descendant of the house of Baden.

While on my side march I saw lying on the ground a beautiful black bearskin with head and claws, which fugitives had had to throwaway. With cries of "hurrah" I took possession of this in the hope of bringing my belongings to Germany, for I had various silver vessels from Moscow which were worth from three to four hundred florins. Besides this, I had silk goods, muslin, etc., such as I was able to take in abundance from the stalled. wagons. Nevertheless, all this came to nothing. The retreat led through Kochanova, Toloczin, Krupky, Bobr, and Liecnize to Borissov. In the bustle by day and by night that hardly let me rest or sleep even a few hours in four or five nights, my horse, which was tied to my arm by a strap, was cut off and led away unnoticed. Since I was always accustomed to pulling on the strap on waking up to see whether my horse was still there, I pulled and this time felt no horse. I jumped up-and now what? I thought to myself, even if I had the whole night to spend looking, only a miracle could lead me to my horse, and the likelihood was all the more uncertain if my horse was already on the march. However, I had to do something. I ran left and right, back and forth; and, whenever I tried to run close to a horse, my life was endangered by whipping and beating, for one could not take enough precaution against theft and robbery: usually one of those sitting by the fire had to keep watch. All at once I saw my "Koniak" standing before a chapel door with his strap tied to a soldier who was sleeping inside the doorway. Very softly now I in my turn cut the strap and rode toward my fire. I dared not sleep anymore, I thought, so that if my horse lover returned I could speak with him....

This night I came by chance upon a comrade from B. by the name of Sch. This was the third man from my district whom I met on the way from Smolensk to Moscow and back to this place. An officer also had this man with him as a faithful friend, for he no longer could be distinguished as "Johan" or servant [?]. Indeed, every soldier was like an officer now, since

Army of Italy - IV Corps - under Prince Eugene at the Battle of Ostrovno, July 26th 1812.

none of the uniforms showed any distinction in rank and no superior could command a private. Officers were beaten away from the fire just as privates were whenever they tried to press forward without merited claim. Only mutual support still procured true friendship. This aforesaid countryman, whom I had once liked so well, still had some rice from Moscow, though only a handful. Along with this, I had a little piece of meat which I cut off next to the ears from a dog's pelt with the whole head on it that lay not far from our fire. Just to give the water flavor and to warm our stomachs, we boiled the two together. Now, when it was only half cooked, we started eating; and, although the meat already stunk a good deal and there was no salt with it, we devoured everything with the best appetite, feeling ourselves lucky to have for once obtained something warm.

Some time before the departure, he said to me, "I had a loaf of bread for my master. You have taken it from me." This was a pain to my feelings which I can never in my life forget. It is noteworthy how an opinion which is entirely false can turn a friend into a scoundrel and change him into a shameful caricature of a human being on account of a bit of bread. Here I saw truly how low reason had sunk with us: our brains were frozen, and there was no feeling left. I swore and said, "Comrade, you are wrong. I have not seen or taken any bread. I would rather give you bread than take it." It did no good. He remained firm in his opinion, and death soon found him.

Before I came to Borissov, we bivouacked behind a forest around eleven o'clock at night, and it seemed as though the Russians had

Hard fighting on the right flank.
Noon at the Battle of Ostrovno, July 26th 1812

Grande Armée - Light Horse Lancers in Society Dress
Carle Vernet, La Grande Armée de 1812

surrounded us entirely, for the cannonades thundered upon us from all sides, and it was necessary to retreat hurriedly until the enemy gave up from weariness. Everyone among us let loose with slugging, hitting, and chasing, as if we were enemies among ourselves. Every time in bivouac the Germans joined together and made the fires in groups I was also included. They were mostly Württemberg sergeants and soldiers who joined with me at the fire; and here each one fried the horse meat which he had cut off laboriously along the way often with scuffling and slugging; for, as soon as a horse plunged and did not get up immediately, men fell upon it in heaps and often cut at it alive from all sides. The meat, unfortunately, was very lean, and the only skin with a little red meat could be wrested away. Each of us stuck his piece on a stick or saber, burned off the hair in the fire, and waited until the outside was burned black. Then

The Viceroy reacts to Russian manoeuvres.
Afternoon at the battle of Ostrovno, July 26th 1812.

the piece was bitten off all around and stuck into the fire again. One seldom had time for boiling, and not one among twenty men had a pot.

When the night meal was ended here, we all lay down, and I went to sleep. My horse was tied to my arm as was my custom. In a short time one of my sincere comrades cried, "You, look after your horse so that it won't be stolen." I said, "It's here all right." I was not awakened again the second time. My countrymen cut the strap and sneaked away. Then I woke up to find myself forsaken. "God," I thought, "who is it that can save me? What is to be done? Mine and my master's possessions I cannot bring any farther. I cannot carry even my fur because of my weakness, and I must freeze to death without it." These thoughts made me despondent, and increasing pain consumed my body. Now I had to risk something even if my life should be lost; besides, it was already half gone, I thought. Only about a hundred paces away lay the French Cuirassier Guards who earlier had forcibly taken my coffee and sugar loaf while in camp. I will risk taking a horse! I crept near the front, observing which of the men did not move and might be sleeping, cut off a strap, and came away with a very large black horse. I went to a place some distance away where no one was about, then ran hurriedly to get my luggage, laid it on, and went on without delay. Indeed, I thought, if only the owner will not see me! Because of this fear, I later traded off the horse.

Before daylight, as I rode thoughtfully along, I heard my master again, Major von Schaumberg. I called him by name, whereupon he heartily rejoiced and said, "Now we are together again." He told of his preservation until now, and I also told him of mine. He was particularly glad about my care for his luggage and about my re conquest of a horse. After we came to Borissov, we bivouacked again. We came to a lumberyard and built a fire there. When the major had become somewhat warm, his "subjects" plagued him with unusual wickedness, and for this reason he asked me to kill the tormentors in his shirt collar. I did it; but, when I had his collar open, his raw flesh showed forth where the greedy beasts had gnawed in. I had to turn my eyes away with abhorrence and reassure the master that I saw nothing, telling him that my eyes hurt so much from the smoke that I could not see anything. These pests, however, were no less to be found on me, thousands of them. However, because of my constant restlessness they could not get to the point of forcing me to treat them with flesh. Besides, I remembered the saying, "Lice stay on healthy people only," and I did not count this a plague in view of the greater one. As I walked about within the court, I saw about twenty dead cows which must have died from hunger and cold. When I tried to cut something off from them with my saber, they were all frozen as hard as a rock, and only with the greatest effort did I finally rip a belly open. Since I could cut or tear nothing loose but the entrails, I took the tallow and supplied myself with a goodly amount of it. Each time I would stick a little of this tallow on my saber and let it get just hot enough in the fire for the greatest part of it to remain unmelted, and I would eat one piece after another with the greatest eagerness. What I had heard before - namely, that tallow-eating drove sleep away, I now found to be true. For about fourteen days I had tallow, which I always ate only in the greatest emergency and which I thriftily saved; and, truly, sleep did not bother me any more: I could always be active then throughout the night and could forage for myself and my horse in various ways.

It was November 25, 1812, when we reached Borissov. Now the march went toward the Beresina River, where the indescribable horror of all possible plagues awaited us. On the way I met one of my countrymen, by the name of Brenner, who had served with the Light Horse Regiment. He came toward me completely wet and half frozen, and we greeted each other. Brenner said that the night before he and his horse had been caught

The Emperor arrives in the afternoon at the Battle of Ostrovno, July 26th 1812

and plundered but that he had taken to flight again and had come through a river which was not frozen. Now, he said, he was near death from freezing and starvation. This good, noble soldier had run into me not far from Smolensk with a little loaf of bread weighing about two pounds and had asked me whether I wanted a piece of bread, saying that this was his last supply. "However, because you have nothing at all, I will share it with you." He had dismounted, laid the bread on the ground, and cut it in two with his saber. "Dear, good friend," I had replied, "you treat me like a brother. I will not forget as long as I live this good deed of yours but will rather repay you many times if we live!" He had then a Russian horse, a huge dun, mounted it, and each of us had to work his way through, facing his own dangers. This second meeting, with both of us in the most miserable condition because no aid was available, caused a pang in my

Murat, King of Naples, the Prince and Napoleon observing the Russian dispositions, revise the order of battle. Evening at the Battle of Ostrovno, July 26th 1812.

heart which sank in me unforgettably. Both of us were again separated, and death overtook him.

When we came nearer the Beresina River, there was a place where Napoleon ordered his pack horses to be unharnessed and where he ate. He watched his army pass by in the most wretched condition. What he may have felt in his heart is impossible to surmise. His outward appearance seemed indifferent and unconcerned over the wretchedness of his soldiers; only ambition and lost honor may have made themselves felt in his heart; and, although the French and Allies shouted into his ears many oaths and curses about his own guilty person, he was still able to listen to them unmoved. After his Guard had already disbanded and he was almost abandoned, he collected a voluntary corps at Dubrovna which was enrolled with many promises and received the name of "Holy Squadron." After a short time, however, this existed in name only, for the enemy reduced even them to nothing.

In this region we came to a half-burnt village away from the road, in which a cellar was found under a mansion. We sought for potatoes, and I also pressed down the broad stairway, although the cellar was already half filled with people. When I was at the bottom of the steps, the screaming began under my feet. Everyone crowded in, and none could get out. Here people were trampled to death and suffocated; those who wanted to stoop down for something were bowled over by those standing and had to be stepped upon. In spite of the murderous shrieking and frightful groaning, the pressure from outside increased; the poor, deathly weak men who fell had to lie there until dead under the feet of their own comrades. When I reflected on the murderous shrieking, I gave up pushing into the cellar, and I thought in cold fear: how will I get out again? I pressed flat against the wall so that it afforded me shelter and pushed myself vigorously little by little up the steps; this was almost impossible with others treading on my long coat. In the village of Sembin, where Napoleon ate, there was a burned house, under which was a low, timber-covered cellar with a small entrance from the outside. Here again, as potatoes and the like were being hunted for, suddenly the beams fell in and those who were inside and were not entirely burned up or suffocated were jumping about with burned clothes, screaming, whimpering, and freezing to death in terrible pain.

When I had gone somewhat farther from that place, I met a man who had a sack of raw bran in which there was hardly a dust of flour. I begged him ceaselessly to sell me a little of the bran, pressing a silver ruble into his hand; so he put a few handfuls in my little cloth, although very unwillingly, whereupon I happily continued on my journey. When I and my master came closer to the Beresina, we camped on a near-by hill, and by contributing wood I obtained a place at a fire. I immediately mixed some snow with my bran; balled it together into. a lump about the size of my fist, which because of its brittleness fell into three or four pieces again in the fire; and allowed it to heat red on the outside in order to obtain something like bread from the inside; and I and my master ate it all with the heartiest appetite.

After a time, from about two till four o'clock in the afternoon, the Russians pressed nearer and nearer from every side, and the murdering and torturing seemed about to annihilate everyone. Although our army used a hill, on which what was left of our artillery was placed, and fired at the enemy as much as possible, the question was: what chance was there of rescue? That day we expected that everyone must be captured,

The attack is halted as Napoleon reconnoitres the terrain and awaits the arrival of reinforcements, on the evening of the Battle of Ostrovno, July 26th 1812.

THE RUSSIAN GENERAL
MICHAIL ILLARIONOVICH KUTUZOV
(1745 - 1813),
Painted by R.M. Volkov in 1813.

killed, or thrown into the Water. Everyone thought that his last hour had come, and everyone was expecting it; but, since the ridge was held by the French artillery, only cannon and howitzer balls could snatch away a part of the men. There was no hospital for the wounded; they died also of hunger, thirst, cold, and despair, uttering complaints and curses with their last breath. Also our sick, who had been conveyed to this point in wagons and consisted almost entirely of officers, were left to themselves; and only deathly white faces and stiffened hands stretched toward us.

When the cannonade had abated somewhat, I and my master set out and rode down the stream for about half an hour to where there was a village with several unburned houses. Here was also the general staff of Württemberg. In the hiding places here, I sought for something to eat at night; with this purpose I lighted candles that I had found; and I did find some cabbage ("Kapusk") which looked green, spotted, and like rubbish. I placed it over a fire and cooked it for about half an hour. All at once cannon balls crashed into the village, and with a wild cheer the enemy sprang upon us. With all the speed we succeeded in escaping, since we mounted and rode away as fast as possible. I couldn't leave my pot of cabbage behind, to be sure, but held it firmly in my arms on the horse, and the fear that I might lose my half-cooked meal made me forget entirely the bullets which were flying by. When we were a little distance from the place, my master and I reached our hands into the pot and ate our cabbage ("Kapuska") in haste with our fingers. Neither could leave his hands bare because of the cold, and because of our hunger and the cold we vied with each other in grabbing swiftly into the warm pot, and the only meal for the entire day was at an end again in short time.

When it became day again, we stood near the stream approximately a thousand paces from the two bridges, which were built of wood near each other. These bridges had the structure of sloping saw-horses suspended like trestles on shallow-sunk piles; on these lay long stringers and across them only bridge ties, which were not fastened down. However, one could not see the bridges because of the crowd of people, horses, and wagons. Everyone crowded together into a solid mass, and nowhere could one see a way out or a means of rescue. From morning till night we stood unprotected from cannonballs and grenades which the Russians hurled at us from two sides. At each blow from three to five men were struck to the ground, and yet no one was able to move a step to get out of the path of the cannonballs. Only by the filling up of the space where a cannonball made room could one make a little progress forward. All the powder wagons also stood in the crowd; many of these were ignited by the grenades, killing hundreds of people and horses standing about them.

I had a horse to ride and one to lead. The horse I led I was soon forced to let go, and I had to kneel on the one which I rode in order not to have my feet crushed off, for everything was so closely packed that in a quarter of an hour one could move only four or five steps forward. To be on foot was to lose all hope of rescue. Indeed, whoever did not have a good horse could not help falling over the horses and people lying about in masses. Everyone was screaming under the feet of the horses, and everywhere was the cry, "Shoot me or stab me to death!" The fallen

Before Vitepsk, the French roll up the Russian left flank, noon July 27th 1812

horses struck off their feet many of those still standing. It was only by a miracle that anyone was saved.

In the crowd the major and I held fast to one another; and, as far as it was possible, I frequently caused my horse to rear up, whereby he came down again about one step further forward. I marveled at the intelligence with which this animal sought to save us. Then evening came, and despair steadily increased. Thousands swam into the river with horses, but no one ever came out again; thousands of others who were near the water were pushed in, and the stream was like a sheep dip where the heads of men and horses bobbed up and down and disappeared.

Finally, toward four o'clock in the evening, when it was almost dark, I came to the bridge. Here I saw only one bridge, the second having been shot away. Now it is with horror, but at that time it was with a dull,

Before Vitepsk, the Viceroy's shelter, July 27th 1812.

indifferent feeling, that I looked at the masses of horses and people which lay dead, piled high upon the bridge. Only "Straight ahead and in the middle!" must be the resolution. "Here in the water is your grave; beyond the bridge is the continuation of a wretched life. The decision will be made on the bridge!" Now I kept myself constantly in the middle. The major and I could aid one another; and so amid a hundred blows of sabers we came to the bridge, where not a plank was visible because of the dead men and horses; and, although on reaching the bridge the people fell in masses thirty paces to the right and to the left, we came through to the firm land.

The fact that the bridge was covered with horses and men was not due to shooting and falling alone but also to the bridge ties, which were not fastened on this structure. The horses stepped through between them with their feet and so could not help falling, until no plank was left movable on account of the weight of the bodies. For where such a timber still could move, it was torn out of place by the falling horses, and a sort of trap was prepared for the following horse. Indeed, one must say that the weight of the dead bodies was the salvation of those riding across; for, without their load, the cannon would have caused the destruction of the bridge too soon.

By the time I was in safety, it had grown dark, and I did not know where the highway was. I lay down somewhat to the left of the road in a little clump of bushes and tied the horses to my foot. The major sent a Pole after water with a kettle bought the day before and also gave him a piece of money, but the man and the kettle were never seen again, and we both had to eat the snow for our thirst. There were now so few people around that in our quiet place it seemed as though everyone had been struck dead. The cannon fire also ceased, and the bridge had really sunk, too. Horrible was the lot of the people who still were on the other side: hunger, cold, and water brought them to their death.

When in the night a little moonlight appeared, I set out upon the march again, for, on account of the cramps in my feet, I could not lie still for a quarter of an hour. Again and again I turned from one side to the other, and in the end I was frozen stiff with my clothing. Only by marching did I overcome freezing. November 26, 27, and 28.

We both hurried farther along the highway; and, being daily without bread and shelter, I thought of my friends at home and compared my misery and approaching end with my former life of plenty. I remembered a common saying at home, "A campaign is always made out to be worse than it was." With this common notion I consoled myself, thinking: "It's well that you, my beloved kindred and friends, know nothing of my condition, for it would only cause you pain, and it would be of no use to me." Yes, I thanked the Creator that only I and not

my brother, too, was here. Certainly I would have lost my brother or seen him die without aid, which would have killed me as well.

I could look with indifference at the people falling by the hundreds, although the impact upon the ice bashed their heads. I could look at their rising and falling again, their dull moaning and whining, and the wringing and clenching of their hands. The ice and snow sticking in , their mouths was frightful. Nevertheless, I had no feeling of pity. Only my friends were in my thoughts.

During this month the cold became worse daily. I had to be more and more careful of myself in order to keep from freezing; also keeping my horse and the major's from starving kept me busy day and night. I rode sometimes to the right and sometimes to the left in order to find a village, and load some straw or unthreshed sheaves on my horse and sit on top of them. Sitting on the straw was absolutely necessary, for otherwise it would have been stolen or torn away by the other horses.

Thus I came to Smorgoni, always keeping nearly in the middle of the army, which, however, more nearly resembled a troop of beggar Jews than one of soldiers. Here I met again, to my astonishment, well-organized regiments which came from Danzig to our support. There were two regiments of Poles who had just come back from Spain; they threw in their lot with us. A few troops came also from Württemberg, to join the Seventh Regiment, which had already been routed, likewise troops from the depot; but I did not hear of an acquaintance. Moreover, here in this region Napoleon had left us and fled with the fresh reserve troops, hurrying home ahead of the army. The general cry was, "Save himself who can." However, Murat had taken over the command of the army and remained

The aftermath, August 1812

Smolensk from the north, August 19th 1812

with us. On the journey from the Beresina through Plechnizi, Slaiski, Molodetschno, and Smorgoni, I had lost the. major a second time, and not until a week later did I meet him with a Württemberg captain by the name of Frost. Both were happy to have me as their attendant again.

When we approached Vilna, the cold increased still more; everyone had been forced to camp out in the snow without shelter since we had left Moscow. At night one could really see how much space the army still occupied. The fires were always visible about a two hours' march in length and about an hour's in breadth. Because of the fire and cold, the sky was a glowing red, which was increased by the burning buildings standing off the highway. Many people were almost blinded by the smoke, which did not rise because of the cold, and still others became dizzy. All our misery was reaching its climax.

When I was still a three days' journey from Vilna, about three o'clock in the afternoon the major gave me his horse, on which his coat was lying, and said that I should go just a little slowly, since he wanted to walk out a little way; and so I soon stopped and waited for him. Captain Frost and his attendant were also with me and waited, but no major came back. We waited a whole hour, and in vain. I was only too certain that he had frozen to death. What had probably happened to him was that he had not been able to put on his pulled-down trousers again because of the cold. It had been the fate of many hundreds, when they had sat down because of weakness or neccessity, that their clothing had been brutally torn from them and, where they could not defend themselves, they froze to death naked. Someone had tried this on me also, but I drove him away with a rather hard kick.

While I and the captain were still waiting for our major, the cold gripped me so terribly that I felt half-numbed. I said then, "Captain, if you still wish to wait, I'll turn the major's horse over to you. I feel that I am about to freeze, and so I am going." Then the captain left, too, and the night showed us a burning hamlet about half a mile away to the left of the highway. We hurried toward it and warmed ourselves there till about five o'clock in the morning. Then I heard cheering and a terrible noise on the highway, to which I called the captain's attention: "Let's get away; the Russians must be on the highway."

The captain did not wish to leave the fire, and only after strong argument did he come with me. I then had a horse for myself, in addition to the major's horse, and took another which stood saddled by the fire. On account of the cold I did not ride but led these three horses by the straps, going toward the highway. Thus we came into the midst of the enemy on the highway. I did not have enough strength to mount my horse, because I could not set my feet, which were bound in rags, in the stirrups and without the use of stirrups I was too weak to mount. I trotted as well as I could with the horses. The Russians called to us that they would pardon us, thinking that we would stop and surrender. We called back, "Comrade, pardon us," but we did not stop. Then the Cossacks rode first at the captain and his attendant and beat them over the heads; both fell from their horses. One also rode at me from the left and thrust his lance into my side, and so then I sprang to the other side of the horses. At the same time, however, a second Cossack thrust his lance at my neck. I let the two horses go, pulled the nearest one aside, threw myself into the snow and the horse on top of me; so both of us lay as if lifeless in the snow a little off from the road. Here I rested, lying in wait with no feeling of hunger or cold. I only kept my eyes and ears fixed on the enemy in order to get an opportunity to flee. I saw the beating and pushing, and heard the whining which continued around me and could not risk making a move. All who still were standing upright were knocked down or killed. Little by little the road was emptied, since the Cossacks in front pursued the army and those behind retreated with the captives. It was my good fortune that no Cossack could plunder or expose his hands because of the cold. They had their gloves on even while thrusting their lances; that is why the first stroke at me had only passed through some of my clothes, and even the second at my neck had not injured the flesh.

After a quarter of an hour had passed, I saw it clear around me, and immediately worked myself from beneath the horse, and ran straight to the nearest wild heaths and woods on the right side of the highway. Nevertheless, in the midst of my flight I picked up a kettle with a bail on it, inside of which lay peas and a package of muslin. While I was running along in 15 inches of snow, having escaped the danger, I thought of my rescue and thanked God for His fatherly providence - all the more so since I had obtained these peas and at the same time a cooking utensil in this lonely expanse, as though prepared by God. There was always a general need for cooking utensils, and only about one man in a hundred was provided with any. Nearly always I had to eat my horse meat, hempseed, rye, and raw grains uncooked. First of all, one had no fire; secondly, no water, having slowly to melt snow; and, finally, no utensils - usually, however, not any of all these.

In my half-joyful and half-dead condition I worked my way forward on this same day almost an hour and a half, traveling off the highway. Only the rumbling and clanging of iron tires, together with the cries of people, guided me unfailingly along my way. It grew dark, and I did not need to think: "Where will you sleep?" But as always: "The snow is your bed; and your coat and fur, your cover!" Yet suddenly I saw again a burning village about an hour's journey ahead; so I hurried to get there. When I came near,

Smolensk, August 1812

The soldiers make camp outside Smolensk, August 19th 1812.

I was on my guard until I heard what language was spoken. Since I heard no more Russians, luckily, I ran to the fire. There were some twenty buildings in flames. Here I again met three men from Württemberg, and I passed the night with them.

One of them said, "If you cook your peas and if I may 'eat with you, I will add salt and fat," to which I gladly consented. Even without this offer I would not have been able to see my countrymen go hungry so near my own unusually good dish. The fat was added, and finally we ate. When we had eaten scarcely a few mouthfuls, however, our throats burned and itched so strongly that no one was able to keep on. We examined the fat:

it was soap. The food had to be thrown out, and only our hunger remained, for the peas had all been cooked. We stayed there half the night and then traveled on. The next day and also the third one, I had nothing at all to eat except some beet-juice broth I found once in a wooden tub that had a hole in the middle about three inches wide, which was unfrozen so that I could quench my thirst.

On the evening of the third day I reached the army just outside Vilna. It was in a terrific tumult. I arrived there scarcely before the Russians, who were constantly taking prisoners. Here I stood beside a mass of people who occupied all the hills in front of the city. On account of the horses and the wagons, many of them without living horses, which had piled in front of the city gates, the soldiers could not go ahead. With difficulty and with risk of life, people worked their way over the horses and wagons. Therefore, I decided to go entirely around the city and to come in from the lower side.

I was led to this undertaking by a countryman whom I met there by accident, the son of the old vine grower from Ellwangen, who came to us with the reserves. Having been acquainted with the city before, he led me into it by special paths; but in a short time I lost this good friend, too. Then I crept down a little side street into a house in which there were some Jews. I at once offered them money to get me brandy and bread. However, for my muslin, about ten yards, they offered me only a flask of brandy, about a pint and a half. I did not haggle long, because my hunger urged me to be short. I obtained the brandy, also a piece of bread, for four Polish florins and consumed everything with a ravishing appetite. When the brandy was gone, I extorted another such flask for one silver ruble but no more bread. Because I had drunk three pints of brandy within three hours, many might believe that I became terribly intoxicated, but I was far from that. Although the brandy was a decent grain brandy, I felt very little effect from it in my head, since my stomach and all parts of my body were empty and hollow and there had been no strength there before. Besides, I did not want to waste anything of this pleasure, since in my case it was a question of "Bird, eat or die!"

When the night was half gone, I started on my way so that I would not be at the rear of the army. I made my way into an enclosed court where there were many horses, untied one which was still in regular sleigh harness, and rode out of the city. About half an hour from the city there was a hill where the wagons and horses again were halted. The slipperiness of the road and the smooth horseshoes made climbing up impossible. The horses fell, and the piling up of the wagons blocked the highway so that those on foot had to climb over them. To avoid this tumult, I crossed the stream to the right and went down the valley. An hour's journey below this hill, I rode over a less steep slope back toward the highway. Because I had been so fortunate at Vilna as to obtain not only bread and brandy but also a horse, it was even harder now to face the misery once more. Hunger began again, and the. cold was still just as bad as in the past days. "Truly, how many more nights will you have to endure without shelter and without fire?" I thought again and again. "My friends, how you would love to help me, and how you would long to see me again, but will it be possible?" That is what I was dreaming about all day long.

By the end of December, we reached the Polish border along the Memel River. When I heard that it would be very hard to get through near Kovno, I led my horse up the river and crossed: it was filled high with pieces of ice, really drifting ice. Pieces from 15 to 18 inches thick drifted by, so that it was extremely troublesome to climb through between them. Here the Polish army turned to the left and set out on the highway into Warsaw. I and many other Germans made use of this turn. Everyone believed that the enemy would no longer pursue the Poles on this route,

Italian Guards around a fire, in front of Smolensk, August 20th 1812

and, therefore, one would be safe; but in their eagerness to rob and plunder the enemy did not stop even here. Even the Poles themselves frequently robbed and plundered the Germans and . French, as I found out the same evening.

That evening a troop of riders rode up to me and said, "Comrade, stay with us!" I ·said, "It's all right with me." When we had gone a little further, they attacked some of the soldiers and took their horses and whatever they had. When I saw this, I turned my horse and rode back as swiftly as possible. They did not catch me again, since just then there approached a troop of Westphalian infantry, which I joined. I expected to continue to travel with these. When it grew dark, however, we looked for

Prince Eugene near the River Vopp, August 25th 1812.

a village, but we did not see one. Finally, some lights blinked from the other side of the Memel. We decided to cross back, for hunger and cold made us not so afraid of danger, and we believed besides that the enemy was far away.

It really was a village. Here, for the first time since we had left Moscow, I came into a decent house, where we were warm and could have bread and brandy for our money. There were ten of us, and the villagers did not seem to be dangerous. At last, about ten o'clock, two peasants asked for bullets, telling us that they were going rabbit-hunting.

The Westphalians still had rifles and powder, and they even gave them bullets. Hardly an hour had passed before a troop of peasants stormed in, seized those who lay on the floor, and took their rifles from them. I saw no chance for help and considered besides that these were Russian peasants, who were still brutal enough to do murder.

The lights were extinguished; and in an instant I took my hat under my fur and went out the door, took my horse which was standing tied and unbridled near the door, and rode away from the village over fences and snowdrifts without following any set course, so that I and my horse fell one time after another. Sometimes I fell beneath him and sometimes on top of him.

Now I was free and left to myself again. As soon as I noticed a trail, I rode as fast as t could, for the noise in the village was so great that I believed I might still be overtaken. I rode as quickly as possible over the cracks in the ice across the Memel River in order to get to the Polish side again. The whole night now I hurried to find a village where people from the army were to be found again. Finally early in the morning, I came into a little town which was crowded with Germans, Frenchmen, and Poles. Nevertheless, I was able to get some bread.

From the Memel River to Moscow and back from there to here, I had not obtained any bread, nor could I buy it except at Vilna; and now there was an end to horse meat. I still had twenty rubles in my pocket with which I hoped to satisfy my future wants. It is true at the time of my capture I had lost silver and silk worth four or five hundred florins besides the three horses and the remaining baggage of the major. However, I did not miss this particularly, since I had saved my life. The indifference toward money was so great with me that at a point four days' journey from

Vilna I did not touch a cart loaded with money which lay on the ground so broken up that the little coin barrels were rolling out. Only a few soldiers had taken any of it when I rode by. There were two reasons, though, why this money had no attraction any longer. It was nearly impossible for me to expose my hands, which were so stiff at the time that I could not feel or take hold of anything with them. I also was eager to get on so as not to be captured at the rear. This money wagon was abandoned as carelessly as any other wagon and the traces cut off. Then if the horses were still there and could be used, the men mounted them and rode on.

I hurried on, therefore, and took the highway between Königsberg and Warsaw to Thorn, where the road was thronged every day with Germans and Frenchmen. Until now there had been no thought of lodgings, nor could victuals be obtained except with money or force. One day along the road I came to a nobleman's manor-house at which I asked for bread and obtained not only bread but also butter and brandy, for there was a house servant there who could speak German. He asked me my nationality and the name of the town or village where my home was. I told him everything, that I was a Catholic and that the late sovereign of my country had been a prince of the King of Poland. This pleased the man immensely, because when the Polish people knew that one was a Catholic they esteemed him much above others. Then I was given also several things to eat along the way; but, when I looked for my horse, it was already gone. Only as a particular favor on the part of the nobleman did I get it again. Nearly everyone who came along alone with a horse had it taken from him.

Several days later, while I once more drank a glass of brandy in an inn, having tied my horse in front of the door, it was stolen from me. All my searching in houses and stables was useless, and so I was set on my own feet again. Until now my feet had been wrapped with woolen cloth over my shoes, but because of the weight this was a hindrance to walking. Now, every morning as soon as I was outdoors, it was necessary to run energetically for an hour along the way. I thought it would be impossible to keep my feet from freezing.

Then with eight German comrades I proceeded toward Ortelsburg, where the road led through a wood that it took almost three hours to journey through. In this region the Poles had formed robber bands wearing Cossack's outfits with sabers, pistols, and other arms. A gang of these actually came and grabbed me, one at the right, one at the left, the third setting a saber against my breast. My comrades ahead remained unassailed, because they looked somewhat more like beggar Jews than I.

Chaos ensues while crossing the Vopp, August 25th 1812

The Battle of Borodino, 7th September 1812
1822 by Louis Lejeune

Now the robbers tore off my fur, coat, cape, vests, and my head cloths; threw me to the ground; and were about to pull off my boots, too. In the meantime they found my money, to the amount of 18 rubles, in my cape pocket. This was my salvation: had they not found the money, I would have been left to freeze to death unclothed. As it was, however, they threw down the coat and the cape again along with one of the two vests and traveled off with the money, the fur, the other vest, and two head cloths. During this time my comrades kept hidden in the distance; and, when they saw that 1 was set free, they came running back and dressed me, for I was so stiff that I was not in a condition to dress myself.

That same evening I came to Ortelsburg and for the first time was given regular quarters. From this city I went on to Niklawi [Mlava?] and at that place received quarters again. It was just Christmas Eve, a date I would not have known if I had not learned it from the landlord. Here I also washed myself for the first time, but I could not rid myself of the lice, or rather of my "sovereigns," because if I had murdered as many as a thousand then the many other thousands would have taken revenge on me. For this reason, I did not undertake an attack on them...

The washing of my hands and face proceeded very slowly because the crusts on my hands, ears, and nose had grown like fir-bark, with cracks and coal black scales. My face resembled that of a heavily bearded Russian peasant; and, when I looked into the mirror, I was astonished myself at the strange appearance of my face. I washed, then, for an hour with hot water and soap. However, I felt I had only become somewhat smoother and lighter, but I could not notice any removal of the blackness and the scales. Only where I had not been shaving did a somewhat lighter

Count Wittgenstein, Colonel of a Bavarian light cavalry regiment.
Of his regiment, only 30 men and two officers were fit for duty, the rest were either killed or wounded. They were not alone, a total of 43 generals were killed or wounded at Borodino, a Pyrrhic victory if there ever was one. September 7th 1812.

skin appear.

In this city, as in all Poland, there were also newly established regiments which had been enlisted for the reenforcement of our army. These people were on horseback, armed with lances, and had on thick coats and clothing in which hardly any of them could move about. I saw several who made a desperate effort to mount a horse, only to fall down again on the other side when they thought themselves up.

As we were departing the next day, the gate toward Thorn and Warsaw was barricaded against us, and everyone was supposed to go back to Königsberg according to the orders of the commandant of the city. This commandant acted on orders. However, we knew the condition of the army better. We were hardly outside the Königsberg gate when we all marched to the left again toward the Thorn highway, in order not to run into the midst of the enemy near Königsberg. Indeed, it cost us enough exertion to get to Thorn before the Russians; with a delay of another two days, it would not have been possible.

On the way we met a column of Bavarians who were en route from Königsberg to the gathering place at Plock. They told us the news that the Würtembergers, too, were gathering in Thorn and that the Germans all had permission to go home. This report strengthened my spirits again, since I had always thought that at the Vistula the army would take up its station and be reorganized and, therefore, that no one would get home or be discharged before another two years or so even if all should go well. I had been convinced of this by the enlisting in Poland.

Finally I came to Thorn; and my only silver ruble, which had escaped notice in my little watch pocket at the time I was plundered, was spent. Here I went to the town hall to obtain quarters, but could not get in on account of the mob. By chance a German soldier came along and said that on this street at a certain number there lived a commissioner from

Imperial Guard Grenadiers near Mojaisk as Napoleon advances on Moscow up the road
from Smolensk while Prince Poniatowski of V Corps advances via the Kaluga road.
The Viceroy of IV Corps (left flank) moved along the Zvenigorod road towards Moscow.
September 10th 1812.

Württemberg and that he would give out passports and travel money. I presented myself immediately and obtained a five-franc thaler and a pass for the third convoy to Inowrazlav. Hence I was one of the last to come to Thorn. The same night I lodged in a house and bought some bread and wine, for free quarters were not to be thought of. One could scarcely creep along the streets on account of the throngs of people. Early in the morning I traveled across the bridge and saw with astonishment that the city during this year of war had been developed into an important fortress. However, they had used only wooden walls and sand around the high walls. I now grew weaker and weaker, and only with great exertion did I reach the city of [Inowr]azlav. Here I reached the third convoy of our people and presented myself immediately to the commander, who asked, "Where are you from?" "From the army," was my answer. "So you are also one of those Moscow bums," he retorted, and that was the welcome at my return.

I was given arms and had to guard the park that same night. Spending this night in the cold again gave me the fever. The next day I was even forced to continue my way on foot alone, but toward evening it became impossible. Either to die on the way or to go off to a village seen from the highway - that was my only choice. I decided then to go into the village. Here I went into a room and immediately lay down on the floor, where the fever shook me frightfully. The people there wanted to give me whiskey and something to eat, but I could drink nothing but water, and all those who looked at me made gestures of hopelessness. I naturally could not understand their conversation, but I could plainly feel their pity. In the morning I gathered together my last strength, left my arms behind because of my weakness; and only toward evening did I arrive in the station-town two hours away, where I found my convoy had already marched off again. I did not want to go to the quartering office first to obtain lodging but lay down in a tavern where there were two Westphalian soldiers who also had the fever at its worst stage. I still could not eat anything but could only drink beer, which I could get there.

The next day a citizen of the town came to the inn, too, and asked what ailed us three. He could speak German. We answered him that each of us had the fever. "The fever?" said he. "I can help you get rid of that." This he really did, sitting down, writing three notes, and saying that each of us should now eat one of them. I, at least, had little faith that such a thing could help. Nevertheless, I ate mine, too; and, when the time came for me to be shaken frightfully again, I waited longer and longer, and actually the fever left not only me but also my other two comrades at the same time. This seemed miraculous and delightful to all of us, and we thanked this good man, without whom certainly none of us would have escaped death. The next day, when we could partake of something to eat again, we obtained a wagon from the police, and I reached the convoy again outside the city of Posen. However, I was no longer able to walk from then on.

The march went on then through Posen toward Crossen. The cold was still extraordinarily great; and, since I could not walk, I froze terribly. Also at night we came into the most miserable huts where even a healthy person had a hard time bearing the cold and the smoke in the rooms with their earthen floors. The convoy consisted of 175 men. However, one or two men of this number were brought dead to their lodgings every day. Our nourishment was still insufficient, and medicine was not to be hoped for. Although the groaning and shrieking on the wagons continued without

Retreat of the French Grande Armée from Moscow,
intercepted by Russian Cossacks, 1812.
Edward Orme, 1813.

The Grande Armée on the outskirts of Moscow. September 20th 1812.

interruption and several who were severely sick were crushed to death by the healthier people, since the space on the wagons was too small, nevertheless the impulse to ;help one another was still quite dulled. As I went through Posen, I met a man from my company - among the 175 men, there was not one from my regiment; much less an acquaintance. When we recognized one another, we kissed each other for joy, and tears flowed down as each one said, "There were five of us common soldiers when we marched out of Moscow; likely we are the last two of these left." This moved us to tears, as I said. This man from my company had been so unfamiliar to me before that I do not even know his name now. When I had to go on, he said that he was well and was just going home but not with the convoy of the sick. I learned at home that he succeeded in doing this. I had asked him, when he went home, to go through Ellwangen and give my friends the news that they could be quite certain of my return, since I was hurrying home in good health and would soon arrive. It was still 250 leagues home; so my homecoming was still uncertain. Nevertheless, hope strengthened me always; so I finally came to Crossen, Torgau, and Leipsic, in which region German life began again, and because of decent eating and warm rooms my strength increased somewhat. In Leipsic especially I had good quarters, and everywhere there was sympathy and decent care for us.

Each of us also obtained a new shirt, and those who could walk the best also got shoes, but I obtained only a shirt. This shirt was of fine white-mangled cloth, yet is was not quite free from little shives, and not until I came to Plauen did I try to put it on. In my quarters there I took off my old shirt and laid it in the warm stove upon a few small pieces of wood in order to murder my evildoers; but, when I looked at it again, I pulled out only the shirtsleeve: all the rest had been burned. Now what else could I do but put on my new shirt? I tried it, put it on and lay down in it, but the shives irritated me so much that I slipped into my clothes without it and exchanged it at my landlady's for a woman's shirt.

During the same night, I also learned there were in our convoy two brothers from Bernlohhof. These were of the Grenadier Company in the regiment of the Crown Prince, and one of them had died that very night. This strange chance, that two brothers who had brought themselves as far as the home stretch by supporting each other should now be separated by the death of one, is surely moving, more so for him who has a brother of his own to remember as I had.

Then the march went through Bayreuth, Nuremberg, Ansbach, and Dinkelsbühl. Everywhere we were quartered without hesitation in towns and villages. Gifts also were given us on the wagons, especially in Dinkelsbühl.

Finally, on February 24, 1813, I arrived here [at Ellwangen J with my extraordinary uniform. For such a long time I had been looking forward to my arrival at home; but, the closer I came, the more my heart pounded at the thought of seeing my friends. I would rather have arrived at nighttime; but it had to be by day, toward three O'clock in the afternoon.

My convoy from [Inowr]azlav to here had left behind 100 dead out of 175 men, and 75 men on a few wagons reached the border. Since people here already knew of the arrival of a third part of the Württemberg army, my brother and my brother-in-law, Herr Wagner, hurried toward Rettstadt to ask about me if they should not meet me. All at once I saw my brother-in-law and my brother. They would not have recognized me, of course, as I looked then; but I called, thrust out my hand, and greeted them. They jumped into the air for joy and pressed my hands, and our hearts alone could feel, for we could not speak. Oh, that all people might know how high the love of friends and relatives can mount through such a chance meeting! One feels in it heavenly joy, the all-wise providence of God, and at the same time the miracle of nature.

So my brother-in-law ran at once with powerful stride, toward the town and announced my arrival to everyone. Thus I made my entrance with a sooty Russian coat, an old round hat, and, under and in my clothing, countless traveling companions, among which were Russians, Poles, Prussians, and Saxons. I stopped off at my very good friend's, the innkeeper's. Everyone wanted to lift me down and lead me, and everyone regarded me as weaker than I really was. However, I stayed only a few minutes in the room before I took off my clothes in the haymow, put on the new ones already provided for me, and washed myself. Only then was I fit for clean company.

Now I also awaited my dear sisters, who did not come in from Rosenberg until the following day and were another object of joy. The

The confusion and despair is evident in the faces of the French.
Moscow, September 20th 1812.

sincere joy of meeting again kindled the love of kindred as a divine flame, and now the wish was fulfilled for which they had shed so many tears and had so often prayed to God.

The next day, on Shrove Thursday, a rest day was observed upon the request of the innkeeper; he brought it about through the city commandant, Alberti, who often came to the tavern. I now had good eating and drinking, but my stomach could not stand many things as yet. I had to be quite careful all the time. On the third day, when we had driven on again, we came to Schorndorf in the evening and were shut into a house together so that we should spread no sickness, for everywhere in Württemberg we were shunned like lepers.

When we came to Waiblingen, the transport was divided, and those who were in better health, of whom I was one, went to Waldenbuch; those whose health was worse went to Vaihingen-on-the-Enz. After a fortnight I was detached to Asperg as a convalescent and was incorporated into the sharpshooters who were stationed there then, and I marched out several times with them. Barely four days had gone by, however, before the fever shook me again, although it did not break out. I ran a high temperature; and my nosebleed grew so bad that for several days a wet cloth had to be put around my head and neck every five or six minutes and the bed had to be arranged for sitting up instead of lying down; but, since my illness got worse, I was examined by the general army physician as to my physical condition, and leave was granted to me on account of my arm, which had been hurt at the time of my capture, having been wrenched somewhat in the shoulder blade and reset. At the same time an invalid pension was also

The sacking of Moscow, September 22nd 1812.

promised me.

When I had grown so weak that I became delirious and everyone doubted that I would recover, I was loaded upon a wagon with several "Russians" and driven to Vaihingen. I was now so weak that I had to be lifted into and off the wagon and I could take nothing any more but drinking water. In Vaihingen I was laid immediately in the room where all were brought who were near death. No medicine or food would stay with me. However, the bleeding had stopped.

Finally, after eight or nine days had passed, I longed for vinegar, and I poured some of it into my soup. These few spoonfuls of soup stayed with me, and now my desire increased for vinegar and lettuce. The lettuce also stayed with me, although I had to take it secretly without the doctor's knowing about it. My appetite gradually rose so that I had potato salad, pure vinegar, pork, potatoes and cabbage, and cooked meat from the butcher brought to me secretly, and then I took no more medicine. I could attribute my recovery to nothing else than the bleeding, by which the corrupted blood came from me, and to the vinegar, which washed off the encrusted lining in my body, cleaned my blood, and encouraged my appetite again.

When my relatives and friends heard of my illness, my little or younger sister, greatly worried, came to visit me, in two days traveling thirty hours. All the sick were in the castle, and the fathers and mothers were kept from entering by the guard. All of them had to go away again without being permitted to speak with their sons. This caused my sister great pain, and she could not weep enough about it; yet chance and luck made a secret meeting possible, for my sister waited until the time when Sharpshooter Seybold from Hohenberg came to the post at the outer gate. He gave her permission to speak to me near the castle wall at the left and sent secretly and had someone ask me to come out. When I saw my sister and she saw me, it took a long time for her to stop weeping and to speak. My appearance had frightened her terribly, for I was deathly pale, my coat was full of blood, and my voice, deep and weak; but, when I said that I thought myself out of danger, since I felt almost well and could eat everything, she was somewhat comforted. However, the fear that she might not be allowed to speak with me had made her almost more ill than I thought myself to be. Thus we tarried as loving brother and sister for an hour's time and then parted again with tears.

During a period of two weeks I still had violent, attacks of gout in the soles of my feet as well as a strong headache, and yet I did not take the medicine but always told the physician that I was well now. However, he did not believe me but said that I must have a headache and gout in my feet, in which I agreed with him, but only in my thoughts.

Finally, I was again brought as a convalescent with about 70 men to Waldenbuch to the convalescent hospital and was quartered on the way in a village, but because of the fear of the nervous fever we all had to go to the town hall and were not supposed to go out. This was hard on us, always to be treated like lepers. We went, therefore, into the inns and had some fun. It did not last long, though, until the citizens wanted to storm us, with alarms ringing and with the threat of bringing the militia from Stuttgart if we would not go back to the town hall at once. There was nothing left but to give in and to accept scorn as our reward.

At Waldenbuch Castle I more or less got my strength back, since I bought what I wanted in addition to my regular diet. Then I wrote a letter to Lieutenant Stimmer at Asperg, asking him to help me in getting my promised discharge. This was done, too, since the colonel in the hospital told me that if I wanted to go I could call for my discharge from Herr Stimmer.

At once I went through Stuttgart and toward Asperg; but, as I came to the first village in the direction of Ludwigsburg, I suddenly got such a pain in my foot that I had to walk an hour instead of a quarter hour to get to the village. Several people who saw me and recognized me as a "Russian" - as everyone who had been there was called at that time - gave me presents. Finally I came to the mayor's house and was given a conveyance to Asperg. I obtained my discharge and had myself driven home, where I then in a short time became entirely healthy and well.

A despondent Napoleon, September 22th 1812.

The scorched earth tactics that reduced Moscow to rubble played a large part in the breakdown of discipline in the French forces. Supplies from Moscow were essential for the continuation of the campaign, as the men went hungry discipline broke down as many resorted to looting for to survive. September 20th 1812.

MORE FROM THE SAME SERIES

Most books from the 'Military History from Original Sources' series are edited and endorsed by Emmy Award winning film maker and military historian Bob Carruthers, producer of Discovery Channel's Line of Fire and Weapons of War and BBC's Both Sides of the Line. Long experience and strong editorial control gives the military history enthusiast the ability to buy with confidence. The series advisor is David McWhinnie, producer of the acclaimed Battlefield series for Discovery Channel. David and Bob have co-produced books and films with a wide variety of the UK's leading historians including Professor John Erickson and Dr David Chandler.
Where possible the books draw on rare primary sources to give the military enthusiast new insights into a fascinating subject.

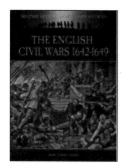

The English Civil Wars

The Zulu Wars

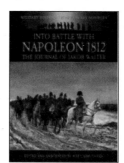

Into Battle with Napoleon 1812

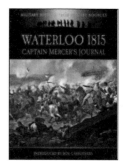

Waterloo 1815

The Anglo-Saxon Chronicle

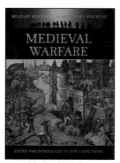

Medieval Warfare

Renaissance Warfare

1914-1918

Sea Battles in the Age of Sail

Sun Tzu - The Art of War

Recollections of the Great War in the Air

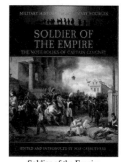

Soldier of the Empire

For more information visit www.pen-and-sword.co.uk